teach®
yourself

vene

teach® yourself

slovene
andrea albretti

revised by
natasha stanič

For over 60 years, more than
50 million people have learnt over
750 subjects the **teach yourself**
way, with impressive results.

be where you want to be
with **teach yourself**

SW09-214
ALB

The publisher has used its best endeavours to ensure that the URLs for external websites referred to in this book are correct and active at the time of going to press. However, the publisher and the author have no responsibility for the websites and can make no guarantee that a site will remain live or that the content will remain relevant, decent or appropriate.

For UK order enquiries: please contact Bookpoint Ltd, 130 Milton Park, Abingdon, Oxon OX14 4SB. Telephone: +44 (0) 1235 827720. Fax: +44 (0) 1235 400454. Lines are open 09.00–17.00, Monday to Saturday, with a 24-hour message answering service. Details about our titles and how to order are available at www.teachyourself.co.uk

For USA order enquiries: please contact McGraw-Hill Customer Services, PO Box 545, Blacklick, OH 43004-0545, USA. Telephone: 1-800-722-4726. Fax: 1-614-755-5645.

For Canada order enquiries: please contact McGraw-Hill Ryerson Ltd, 300 Water St, Whitby, Ontario L1N 9B6, Canada. Telephone: 905 430 5000. Fax: 905 430 5020.

Long renowned as the authoritative source for self-guided learning – with more than 50 million copies sold worldwide – the **teach yourself** series includes over 500 titles in the fields of languages, crafts, hobbies, business, computing and education.

British Library Cataloguing in Publication Data: a catalogue record for this title is available from the British Library.

Library of Congress Catalog Card Number: on file.

First published in UK 1997 by Hodder Arnold, 338 Euston Road, London, NW1 3BH

First published in US 1997 by McGraw-Hill Companies, Inc.

This edition published 2006.

The **teach yourself** name is a registered trade mark of Hodder Headline.

Typeset by Transet Limited, Coventry, England.
Printed in Great Britain for Hodder Education, a division of Hodder Headline, 338 Euston Road, London, NW1 3BH, by Cox & Wyman Ltd, Reading, Berkshire.

Hodder Headline's policy is to use papers that are natural, renewable and recyclable products and made from wood grown in sustainable forests. The logging and manufacturing processes are expected to conform to the environmental regulations of the country of origin.

Impression number   10 9 8 7 6 5 4 3 2 1
Year   2010 2009 2008 2007 2006

contents

introduction

The country

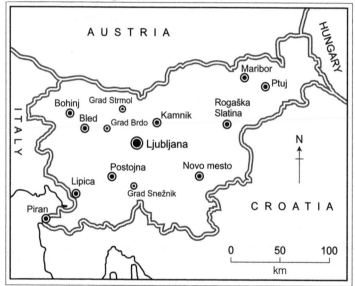

It is with monotonous regularity that many people confuse Slovenia with Slovakia. Yet they are in good company as notably even the president of the USA, George W. Bush, was not too sure on one occasion of the identity of the two countries. A few years ago, he and Vladimir Putin chose Slovenia as the location for their first ever meeting. After the event, in his appraisal of the meeting, George Bush said that he was amazed to see how beautiful Slovakia was.

Although many Slovenes become annoyed at times by this display of geographical illiteracy, there is an excuse for it:

Slovenia, as an independent state after the collapse of the former Yugoslavia, is only 14 years old, has no more than 2 million inhabitants, and is not quite the size of Wales. However, as more and more tourists are recognizing the variety that Slovenia has to offer in both summer and winter, the country is developing a greater identity among ordinary people throughout the world.

The first independent Slovene state dates back to the seventh century AD, when an independent Slavic tribal confederation was established on the Slovene land, quite possibly stretching over a territory three times the size of the present state. Through the turbulent times of the Middle Ages that followed, that independence was lost and regained twice. However, for almost 600 years, from 1335 until 1918, Slovenes were governed by the Habsburgs of the Austro-Hungarian Empire. After the First World War, Slovenia was absorbed into the Serb-dominated kingdom of Yugoslavia, and after the Second World War, it became one of the republics of the Serb-dominated Yugoslav federation, and remained so for 45 years. The events since the early 1990s led to the disintegration of Tito's Yugoslavia and to the final collapse of communist rule worldwide.

Looking at the cultural history of Slovenia, one can see that although a drive for complete Germanization of the Slovenian lands began as far back as the tenth century, the Slovenes were able to preserve their identity, their language and their literature due largely to the intensive educational work done by the clergy. The oldest known Slovene document is a 1,000-year-old manuscript, the publication of the first Slovene books took place in 1550, and the same century saw the first translation of the Bible into Slovene. A century later, the first Slovene newspaper was published. The nineteenth century was a period of Romantic Nationalism, of intensive literary and cultural activities. The poetry of the greatest poet Prešeren, the Slovenian Shakespeare, which is full of longing for political freedom and the unity of all Slovenes, caught the imagination of the nation then and has never let it go.

In 1991, the dream of a thousand years came true. On 26 June, the day after Slovenia withdrew from the Yugoslav federation for good, President Kučan said to the triumphant crowds: 'This evening dreams are allowed. Tomorrow is a new day.'

A further boost to national pride were the events of the war, which started only a few days later with the Yugoslav army marching on Slovenia, and ended just ten days later in a complete defeat of the invading army. Belgrade apparently never expected Slovenia to resist to the degree that it did.

In late December of the same year, Slovenia got a new constitution and the then European Community (EC) formally recognized the country on 15 January 1992. Although the negotiations proper for entry into the European Union (EU) only began in 1998, awareness of the presence and importance of Brussels has been there all the time. There has always been a broad consensus in favour of Slovenian EU membership among the political elite, the relevant political parties, and well-informed individuals. The people on the street, on the other hand, felt no immediate need to indulge in a global vision of united Europe. Their absorbing concern was in the promises given by an ever-increasing number of newly formed political parties, in denationalization of property that had been confiscated under the communist regime, and in the benefits of a fast growing market economy. To this group of people, EU membership appeared somewhat identical to erosion of the very sovereignty that had been won at last after 1,000 years' long struggle. These same views were often heard from the pulpit, although it should be made clear that this was not the official line taken by the hierarchy of the Church in Slovenia, but merely a reflection of the parochial way of thinking among the provincial clergy.

In the early days of Slovenia's independence, its political life was tremendously vibrant. At one time, there was a total of 27 parliamentary and non-parliamentary parties. Political aspirations and ambitions were all-absorbing. As a result, the initial diplomatic relations between Slovenia and the then EC, which began with the 'Cooperation Agreement' in April 1993, passed largely unnoticed. The accession negotiations were officially opened in March 1998 and completed at the December 2002 Copenhagen summit.

By the late 1990s, the political climate in Slovenia had changed. It was beginning to become painfully clear to a great many Slovenes that transition from communism to true democracy was a long and arduous process which could and probably would continue for a generation or two. First, in the political arena the ex-communists were re-establishing themselves under the auspices of political parties of reputable names. They were successful in their attempted come-back because they were the only people who had thorough training and long experience in active politics and diplomatic service. Naturally there have been a few gifted politicians who, although newcomers, have succeeded in establishing themselves on their own merits. Second, the course of denationalization was slow and often hampered by inventive and intentional bureaucracy. Third, in most businesses, the old guard still held a firm control over every form of lucrative enterprise. Lastly, inflation was beginning to rise and the national debt was growing. All these factors seem to have contributed to the rise of political lethargy which was in sharp contrast to the initial euphoria. The two 'Euro-Atlantic' referenda, on EU and North Atlantic Treaty Organization (NATO) accession, which were held on 23 March 2003 simultaneously but as two separate questions, reflected a sense of disappointment with the course of events of the past ten years, and sadness over the dashed hopes and illusions. The voter turn-out at the referenda was only 60 per cent, but the result was a pleasant surprise: an overwhelming majority voted in favour of Slovenia's accession to the EU and NATO. On 1 May 2004, Slovenia joined the EU and has since become a content and valued member to the advantage of all Community members.

Natasha Stanič (2006)

The language

Slovene is one of the southern group of Slavonic languages. In the former Yugoslavia, there were three main languages: Serbo-Croat (spoken in Croatia, Serbia and Bosnia), Macedonian (spoken in Macedonia) and Slovene (spoken in Slovenia). These languages were not only spoken by the people of the respective republics, but were also official languages in those republics, being used in newspapers, theatres, the media and so on. Serbo-Croat was used by the majority of Yugoslavs and was (unofficially) a kind of 'official language' of Yugoslavia. Slovenes heard a lot of it, and so they can understand and speak it. Serbo-Croat speakers were less familiar with Slovene and, apart from recognizing similar words, are less fluent in it.

Slovene is most closely related to the Serbo-Croatian complexity of languages. Around the sixth century, when the migration of the southern Slavs down to the Balkans was taking place, all Yugoslavs spoke variations of the same language. Through the centuries, however, Slovene has developed into a separate and different language. It has its own grammatical structure and a vocabulary which differs from Serbo-Croat. It is not therefore classed as a dialect or variation of Serbo-Croat such as Serbian, Croatian or Bosnian.

For the most part, Slovenia is a mountainous country – almost half of it is covered by forests. Many valleys are separated by high mountains, and for this reason Slovene is split into several dialects, a fact which should not alarm a potential learner since every Slovene is encouraged from early days at school to speak 'standard Slovene'.

Slovene has been resistant to change, which makes learning it quite a challenge. It is a highly inflected language: this means that nouns, pronouns and all adjectives (even numbers!) decline, that is, endings are added to words depending on their function. Do not be surprised if you see a town, country, or your name and surname in a strange form, because these too decline. John Brown can become John**u** Brown**u**, John**a** Brown**a**, John**om** Brown**om**, and these are not misspellings: a certain preposition or grammatical function governs the noun 'John Brown', and his name receives the appropriate suffixes.

In most languages, there are two numbers: singular for one and plural for more than one. Slovene has three: singular, dual and plural. Dual is used when referring to two of anything. This dual number existed in several languages in the past, but has now disappeared. In Slovene it still exists, and it is not merely an academic grammatical structure, but is used all the time. Sentences like 'We are married' or 'They are twins' would sound most odd translated into the plural form in Slovene, since this would imply, for example, that more than two people were married!

Visitors to Slovenia will not have any problems even if they cannot speak a word of Slovene: English, German and Italian are spoken by many people. Nevertheless, if you do have the courage to learn and speak even a little Slovene, it will be much appreciated by the Slovenes, and will make your stay and dealings with the people more interesting and rewarding.

How to use this course

You will notice that each unit in the book follows the same structure. Units are divided into the following sections:

Pogovori (*Dialogues*) A unit starts with one or more dialogues between people talking about everyday matters. These dialogues show you how language is used in a given situation.

Nove besede in izrazi (*New words and expressions*) Words and phrases used in the dialogues are translated after each dialogue.

Ste razumeli? (*Did you understand?*) There are a few comprehension questions to be answered after you have read the dialogue, for you to test whether you understood the language used.

Ste vedeli? (*Did you know?*) In this section you are given some background information on the language and the people who use it. There are also grammatical explanations, which will help you determine why and how particular Slovene words are used in order to put across a particular meaning.

Zapomnite si! (*Remember!*) This is a summary of the most useful expressions for the topic discussed in the unit. Essential phrases you will most definitely need when arriving in Slovenia are translated.

Vaje (*Exercises*) This section is intended for you to practise language patterns and vocabulary as you acquire them.

Pa še to ... (*And something else ...*) Some extra material appears at the end of each unit, which incorporates the structures and the vocabulary explained in the unit. This is designed to extend your comprehension of the language. The vocabulary box after the dialogue or text and notes will help you understand it.

Dialogues or other items marked with ▶ appear on the recording which accompanies this book. To develop good pronunciation and listening skills you are strongly advised to use the recording as much as possible.

At the back of the book there is a *Key to the exercises* section, to which you can refer and check that you got the answers right. You can also refer to the *Appendices* for grammar references. At the end there is a *Slovene–English glossary*, and an *English–Slovene glossary* containing all the words used in the book.

▶ Slovene is easy to spell and to pronounce. Each letter is pronounced separately, and words are spelt as they are pronounced. There are some difficult sounds for English speakers and a few rules to be observed for pronunciation. The alphabet has 25 letters, listed below:

a b c č d e f g h i j k l m n o p r s š t u v z ž

Note the letters that are absent from the English alphabet:

č like **ch** in English **ch**ur**ch**
š like **sh** in English **sh**oes
ž like **s** in English lei**s**ure

You will find q, w, x and y in foreign borrowings.

Vowels

There are five vowels, pronounced as follows:

a as in **a**rtist, c**a**r
e as in p**e**t, b**e**d, **e**xit
i as in m**ea**t, f**ee**ling, b**i**t
o as in h**o**t, p**o**t, n**o**t
u as in ball**oo**n, aftern**oo**n, sp**oo**n

Each syllable contains a vowel, for example:

Do-bro ju-tro, ka-ko vam gre?	*Good morning, how is it going?*
Hva-la do-bro!	*Fine, thanks!*

Consonants

Most consonants sound like the equivalent of English letters. However, note the following:

c like **ts** in English *bits*.

g always hard, as in *lag*.

h can occur anywhere, at the beginning, in the middle or at the end of a word. It is always fully pronounced, like **h** in *home*, never like **h** in *honour* or *honesty*.

j like English **y** in *yes*, *yet*, *yoghurt*. It is not pronounced as in English *job* or *joke*!

l like **l** in *leg* when it comes before a vowel or the consonant **j**, for example: **plača** (*wage*, *salary*), **ljudje** (*people*). Before all other consonants and at the end of words, **l** is pronounced like **w** in *now*, for example: **volk** (*wolf*), **videl** (*saw*), **rekel** (*said*).

r rolled as in Scottish English. It can be a syllable in its own right when it occurs:
  - before a consonant, at the beginning of a word as in **rdeč** (*red*), **rjav** (*brown*)
  - before another consonant, as in **vrtnica** (*rose*)
  - between two consonants, as in **črn** (*black*), **vrt** (*garden*)

šč the combination of these two consonants occurs in a lot of words, for example, **parkirišče**, **kuščar**

v like **v** in *very* when it comes before vowels or **r**, for example: **vino** (*wine*), **vrata** (*door*). Before consonants and at the end of a word it is pronounced like **w** in *now*, for example: **avtobus** (*bus*, *coach*), **avto** (*car*), **ovca** (*sheep*).

Stress

Accents are not marked in Slovene and there is no definite rule about where the stress comes. It can be on the first, second, third or last syllable.

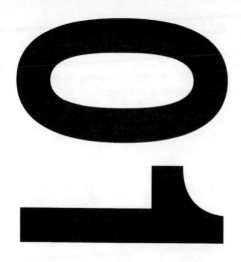

01

kako gre?
how are things?

In this unit you will learn
- how to say who you are
- how to introduce people to each other
- how to greet people in Slovene
- how to use formal and informal modes of address
- how to ask how someone is
- how to ask some simple questions
- what to say in reply in the above situations

Pogovori *(Dialogues)*

▶ Dobro jutro! *(Good morning!)*

Sara is an English student. She has been attending evening classes in Slovene for some time and has arranged to spend a summer in Slovenia with a family. She travels there by train and arrives at Ljubljana railway station. She goes to the counter to get a cup of tea whilst she is waiting.

Natakarica	Dobro jutro!
Sara	Dobro jutro!
Natakarica	Prosim?
Sara	En čaj, prosim.
Natakarica	Izvolite! Tukaj je sladkor in mleko.
Sara	Hvala!

natakarica	*waitress*	**Tukaj je ...**	*here is ...*
dobro jutro	*good morning*	**sladkor**	*sugar*
prosim	*please*	**in**	*and*
en čaj	*one tea*	**mleko**	*milk*
Izvolite!	*Here you are!*	**hvala**	*thanks*

▶ Je to tvoja denarnica? *(Is this your purse?)*

Sara took her tea and went to sit down at a table, but she left her purse on the counter. The waitress reminded her about it.

Natakarica	Oprostite, je to vaša denarnica?
Sara	Prosim?
Natakarica	Je to vaša denarnica?
Sara	Joj! Ja, to je moja denarnica! Najlepša hvala!
Natakarica	Ni za kaj!

oprostite ...	*excuse me ...*
je to ...	*is this ...?*
vaša denarnica	*your purse*
Prosim?	*I beg your pardon?*
ja	*yes*
to je	*this is*
najlepša hvala	*thanks very much*
Ni za kaj!	*Not at all!*

Note. **Denarnica** can mean both *purse* and *wallet*. It comes from the word **denar**, which means *money*.

▶ Me veseli!
(Nice to meet you!)

Sara sees a family come on to the station. The woman walks over to her and says:

Gospa Slak	Oprosti, si ti Sara?
Sara	Ja, jaz sem Sara.
Gospa Slak	Jaz sem gospa Slak. (*They shake hands.*) Me veseli!
Sara	Me veseli!
Gospa Slak	Naj ti predstavim… To je moja hčerka, to je moj sin, in to je moj mož.

gospa	*Mrs*
si ti?	*are you?*
ja	*yes*
jaz sem	*I am*
Me veseli!	*Nice to meet you!*
Naj ti predstavim ...	*Let me introduce you ...*
To je ...	*This is ...*
moja hčerka	*my daughter*
moj sin	*my son*
moj mož	*my husband*

▶ Kako ti je ime? (What's your name?)

Sara meets other members of the family. She exchanges a few words with each of them before she goes home with them.

Gospod Slak	Kako gre?
Sara	Dobro, hvala.
Sara	Kako ti je ime?
Matic	Matic.
Sara	Me veseli!
Matic	Me veseli! Kako se imaš?
Sara	Dobro, hvala.
Sara	Kako ti je ime?
Lara	Lara sem. Kako si?

Sara	Dobro, hvala. In ti?
Lara	Zelo dobro, hvala.

gospod	*Mr*
Kako (ti) gre?	*How are things?*
Dobro, hvala.	*Fine, thanks.*
Kako ti je ime?	*What's your name?*
Kako se imaš?	*How are things?* (lit. 'How are you having yourself?')
Kako si?	*How are you?*
In ti?	*And you?*
Zelo dobro, hvala.	*Very well, thank you.*

Ste razumeli? *(Did you understand?)*

1 a Do you remember the Slovene word for what Sara ordered in the café?
(*Clue*: the number of dots will tell you how many letters the word has.)

. . .

b And what she forgot on the counter?

. . . .

2 Suppose someone says the things below to you: would you answer **a**, **b**, or **c**?

1 Dobro jutro.
  a dobro jutro
  b dober dan
  c dober večer

2 Najlepša hvala!
  a kako si
  b ni za kaj
  c izvolite

3 Kako gre?
  a me veseli
  b kako ti je ime
  c dobro, hvala

Ste vedeli? *(Did you know?)*

1 Pozdravi *(Greetings)*

Dobro jutro, *good morning*, is the first greeting of the day. It is used until about 9.00 or 10.00 a.m., depending on how early your day has started. In general, Slovenes start working a bit earlier than the English, but in recent years this habit has started to change, and working days are becoming more like they are in Europe, where people start and finish later.

From early morning until late in the afternoon people greet each other by saying **dober dan**, *good day*. There is no equivalent to good *afternoon* in Slovene, so you would greet people with **dober dan** all through the day.

In the evening, from about 6.00 or 7.00 p.m. onwards, you say **dober večer**, *good evening*.

When leaving, the standard greeting at any time is **na svidenje**, *good-bye*. It means literally *'until we meet again'*, like the French *au revoir*. Before going to bed, or if you are leaving somewhere late at night, you say **lahko noč**, *good night*.

All of these greetings are answered by repeating the greeting. In many languages you can say or repeat only the second half of the greeting, like saying 'morning', instead of 'good morning'. In Slovene, this would not sound right, you have to say both words.

You will hear a number of less formal greetings used among friends, in particular among young people, such as **živio**, **ciao** (especially in the regions close to Italy), **servus** (a German greeting use in regions close to Austria), or **hay** ... You may also hear others, depending on the fashion.

2 Naj vam predstavim ... *(Let me introduce you ...)*

The phrase **Naj vam predstavim ...** means *let me introduce you* ... You can pause a little and then say: **To je ...** *(this is ...)*, for example:

 To je Sara.   *This is Sara.*

At first introduction, Slovenes usually shake hands and say their name. In more formal situations, you can say your full name.

It is polite to use **gospod** and **gospa** when addressing or referring to adults you do not know. In such instances you would, as in English, say the person's surname rather than their first name, for example:

To je gospod Kovač.	*This is Mr. Kovač.*
To je gospa Dobraj.	*This is Mrs. Dobraj.*
gospod	*Mr*
gospa	*Mrs*
gospodična	*Miss*

In writing you will see the abbreviations for **gospod** as **g.**, for **gospa** as **ga.**, and for **gospodična** as **gdč**. The words **gospod**, **gospa** and **gospodična** are spelt with a small letter unless they occur at the beginning of a sentence.

3 Informal and formal address

In Slovene, as in many other languages, the forms you use when talking to a stranger or to someone you don't know well are different from those you use when talking to friends. When addressing someone whom you are meeting for the first time, or in a formal situation, you would usually use **vi** (*you pl.* like the French *vous*), and when you address friends, members of a family, or children, you use **ti** (*you sg.* like the French *tu*). It is a common slip of children to say **ti** to an elderly person, but their parents will soon tell them: 'You must say **vi** to them.' There are two onomatopoetic verbs derived from **ti** and **vi**: they are **tikati**, meaning to say '*ti*', and vikati, meaning to say '*vi*'. You may be told one of these phrases, so keep them in mind!

Ne me vikati!	*Don't say* vi *to me!*
Mene ni treba vikati!	*There is no need to say* vi *to me!*
Tikaj me!	*Say* ti *to me!*

The tendency today, particularly among young people, is to say **ti**. Colleagues at work usually say **ti** to each other, but in the past there were strict rules about whom you addressed with **vi** and **ti**. The occasion when two people decided to say **ti** to each other was celebrated by drinking from glasses held with linked arms.

Should you wonder which form to use with a particular person, listen to what they say to you, and do likewise.

4 Kako gre? *(How are things?)*

The phrase **Kako gre?** means *How are things?* and you can use it whether you are addressing someone formally or informally.

There are variations on this phrase: you may hear **Kako ti gre?** or **Kako vam gre?** both meaning *How are things with you?* The *you* in the first phrase is familiar, and in the latter, formal.

The question *How are you?* also has two forms: **Kako si?** or **Kako se imaš?** (lit. '*How are you having yourself?*') if you are talking to a friend; and **Kako ste?** or **Kako se imate?** if you are on more formal terms with the person.

The standard answer to all of these questions is equivalent to the English *I'm very well, thank you!* which in Slovene goes: **Dobro, hvala**. You can also say **Ni slabo, hvala**, meaning *Not bad, thank you*. People usually go on to ask the other person how they are, which you do, as in English, by saying *And you?* Again, depending on your relationship with the person you say **In ti?** (if you are on familiar terms) or **In vi?** (if you are on formal terms).

5 Prosim *(Please)*

The English are well known for being polite and using the word 'please' a lot. Slovenes don't have quite the same reputation, but the word 'please' is used a lot in Slovene too: the reason for this is that it can mean many things. Literally, **prosim** means *please* and it is used when you use *please* in English. In addition, it means all the following:

- *I beg your pardon?* indicating that you did not hear what the person said and that you would like them to repeat it
- *Yes, please?* or *How can I help you?* if you are in a bar ordering a drink or in a shop waiting to be served
- *hello* when answering the telephone
- *hello* when answering a knock or ring at the door
- *you're welcome*, as a reply to 'thank you'

6 Hvala *(thank you)*

Hvala means *thank you* or *thanks*. When you are really grateful you say **najlepša hvala**, meaning *many thanks*, or *thank you very much*.

The variations on these are by adding the pronoun *you* in the familiar or polite form as follows:

Hvala vam.	(*polite*)
Hvala ti.	(*familiar*)
Najlepša vam hvala.	(*polite*)
Najlepša ti hvala.	(*familiar*)

When you are given something in a shop or in a restaurant the person will say to you **izvolite**, *here you are*. This, as well as being the formal address, is also the plural, so it is used when addressing more than two people. You also use it if you pass something to someone. If they are your friends, you use the familiar form **izvoli**.

As you have seen above you can reply **hvala**.

Another expression meaning *you're welcome* is **ni za kaj**, lit. *'it's for nothing'*.

7 Slovenska osebna imena *(Slovene personal names)*

Because of its geographical position, a lot of German and Italian names are found in Slovenia. It does not necessarily mean that the person is not Slovene if their surname is **Miler** (German *Müller*), **Ajhmajer** (German *Eichmeier*) or **Sabati, Gaspari** ... Do note, however, that these names have become 'Slovene' in their spelling, i.e they are spelt as they are pronounced. There are also very many surnames ending in **–ič**, like **Žnideršič, Zenič, Majerič**, which come from other republics of former Yugoslavia.

Due to the historical background of Slovenia, it is difficult to say what is actually 'typically Slovene'. This is true not only of names but of culture in general.

Here are some names one could call Slovene:

Surnames	Men's names	Women's names
Novak	Janez	Alenka
Cerar	Matic	Darja
Kotnik	Boštjan	Simona
Jelen	Bojan	Danica
Slak	Matjaž	Majda
Kovač	Gregor	Vesna
Lisjak	Danilo	Špela

When you want to know a person'a name you ask them:

Kako ti je ime?   *What's your name?*
Kako se pišeš?   *What's your surname?*

8 Personal pronouns *(I, you, he, she, etc.)*

jaz	*I*		mi	*we*
ti	*you*		vi	*you* (form.)
on	*he*		oni	*they*
ona	*she*			
ono	*it*			

Personal pronouns in Slovene are used only when you want to emphasize the person, or when it could be ambiguous whom you are referring to. Most of the time they are not used, because the person you are referring to will be clear from the ending of the verb.

9 Glagol 'biti' *(The verb 'to be')*

biti to be

jaz **sem**	*I am*	mi **smo**	*we are*
ti **si**	*you are*	vi **ste**	*you are*
on }	*he* }	oni **so**	*they are*
ona } **je**	*she* } *is*		
ono }	*it* }		

The verb **biti** is irregular, like the English verb '*to be*'. It is best to learn it by heart as soon as you can.

When you want to negate, i.e. to say that something *is not*, the verb **biti** takes negative forms:

jaz **nisem**	*I am not*	mi **nismo**	*we are not*
ti **nisi**	*you are not*	vi **niste**	*you are not*
on }	*he* }	oni **niso**	*they are not*
ona } **ni**	*she* } *is not*		
ono }	*it* }		

10 My, your, his, etc.

Words like *my*, *your*, *his*, etc. are possessive adjectives. They tell us to whom something belongs. Look at these examples:

| To je moja hčerka. | *This is my daughter.* |
| To je moj sin. | *This is my son.* |

Moja and **moj** both mean *my*. You will learn as you work through the book what determines the different endings of these words.

▶ Zapomnite si! *(Remember!)*

How to

- say good morning, good afternoon and good evening:

Dobro jutro.	*Good morning.*
Dober dan.	*Good afternoon.*
Dober večer.	*Good evening.*

- ask how someone is and reply:

Kako gre?	*How are things?*
Kako si (ste)?	*How are you?*
Dobro, hvala!	*Fine, thanks!*
Zelo dobro, hvala!	*Very well, thanks!*

- use some common words for courtesy:

prosim	*please*
hvala	*thanks, thank you*
najlepša hvala	*thank you very much*
ni za kaj	*not at all, you're welcome*

- ask someone's name and give your name:

Kako ti je ime?	*What's your name?*
Ime mi je ...	*My name is ...*
Jaz sem ...	*I am ...*

Vaje *(Exercises)*

1   The following are situations in which you are likely to find yourself in Slovenia. Which of the words or phrases from the box would you use in each?

a It is 8.00 a.m. and you have just arrived at work. How would you greet your colleagues already in the office?

b A Slovene friend of yours has said something, but you didn't hear and would like her to repeat it. Which word would you use?

c You have been invited by a friend to supper. It is 8.00 p.m. and you have arrived at his house. How would you greet the guests already there?

d You are at a bar waiting to be served. The waiter asks you what you'd like. What does he say?

e The waiter has brought you the drink you ordered. What does he say as he gives it to you?

f What do you say when you get the drink?

g An old friend of yours wants to know how things are with you. What does she say?

h You are really grateful for something your friend has done for you. What would you say?

i What is she likely to say in reply?

2 You have just walked into the hotel dining-room to have breakfast. Fill in the missing words in the conversation below:

Dobro —
— jutro. — gre?
—, hvala.

3 When would you use the word **prosim**?

4 **Oprosti … Oprostite …**

a You want to approach a stranger by saying: 'Excuse me …' Which word would you use?

b You are walking down the road with a good friend of yours and you elbow him by mistake. What would you say?

5 Križanka (crossword)

a wallet
b day
c milk
d money
e thanks
f please
g son
h name
i tea
j husband

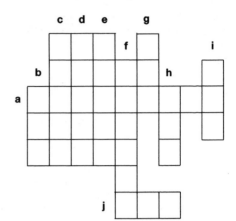

6 Complete the dialogue, using the sentences in the box.

Dober dan.

—

Kako vam gre?

—

Je to vaš sin?

—

Kako ti je ime?

—

Me veseli!

> Ime mi je Matjaž.
> Dober dan.
> Me veseli!
> Ja, to je moj sin.
> Zelo dobro, hvala.

▶ Pa še to ... *(And something else . . .)*

There will be another dialogue at the end of each unit. By studying these dialogues you will be able to add some useful words and phrases to your vocabulary. The vocabulary box at the end of the dialogue will help you.

Sara has arranged to see a friend, Metka, whom she has met in England.

Metka Živio, Sara! Vstopi! Kako se imaš?
Sara Dobro, hvala. Danes je vroče.
Metka Ja, že ves teden je vroče. Za jutri je napovedano poslabšanje vremena. Kaj lahko ponudim? Kavo, čaj, sok ...
Sara Kavo, prosim, in kozarec vode. Žejna sem.

Metka	Samo trenutek! (*She comes back with the drinks.*)
Metka	Izvoli. Tukaj sta sladkor in mleko.
Sara	Hvala.
Metka	Kako ti je všeč Ljubljana?
Sara	Zelo mi je všeč.

Vstopi!	*Come in!* (lit.*enter!*)
danes	*today*
je vroče	*is hot*
že	*already*
ves teden	*all week*
jutri: za jutri	*tomorrow: for tomorrow*
je napovedano	*is forecasted*
poslabšanje vremena	*deterioration of the weather*
Kaj lahko ponudim?	*What can I offer?*
kava	*coffee*
sok	*juice*
kozarec vode	*a glass of water*
Žejna sem.	*I'm thirsty.*
samo trenutek	*just a moment*
Kako ti je všeč ...?	*How do you like...?*
Zelo mi je všec.	*I like it very much.*

02

dobrodošli!

welcome!

In this unit you will learn
- how to say what nationality you are
- how to say what you do for a living
- how to say which languages you speak
- how to count from 1 to 10
- how to ask others about the above topics

▶ Dialogues

Several students have enrolled in a Slovene language course. It is the first day and the teacher, Tanja Kos, enters the classroom and introduces herself.

Tanja Pozdravljeni! Dobrodošli v Sloveniji! Jaz sem Tanja Kos, vaša učiteljica in to je Zmago Kerec, moj asistent. Oba sva Slovenca.

pozdravljeni	*hello*
dobrodošli	*welcome*
vaša učiteljica	*your teacher*
moj asistent	*my assistant*
oba sva Slovenca	*we (two) are both Slovene*

Before the class begins, the students introduce themselves:

Caroline Jaz sem Caroline. Američanka sem. V Sloveniji sem na dopustu. Moj oče je Slovenec. Govorim zelo malo slovensko ampak razumem veliko.

Američanka	*American (woman)*
Slovenija: v Sloveniji	*Slovenia: in Slovenia*
dopust: na dopustu	*holiday: on holiday*
moj oče	*my father*
Slovenec	*Slovene (man)*
govorim	*I speak*
zelo	*very*
malo	*little*
slovensko	*Slovene (language)*
ampak	*but*
razumem	*I understand*
veliko	*a lot*

Klaus Jaz sem Nemec. Ime mi je Klaus. Tukaj sem službeno, že tri mesece. Računovodja sem in delam na banki.

Nemec	*German (man)*
Ime mi je ...	*My name is ...*
služba: službeno	*work: on business*
mesec: tri mesece	*month: three months*
računovodja	*accountant (man)*
delam	*I work*
banka: na banki	*bank: at a/the bank*

Susan Jaz sem Susan. Angležinja sem. V Sloveniji sem z družino, že eno leto. Imam eno hčerko in dva sina. Moj mož dela tukaj, na veleposlaništvu Velike Britanije.

Angležinja	*English* (woman)
družina: z družino	*family: with my family*
leto: že eno leto	*year: one year already*
imam	*I have*
hčerka: eno hčerko	*daughter: one daughter*
sin: dva sina	*son: two sons*
dela	*(he) works*
veleposlaništvo:	*embassy:*
na veleposlaništvu	*at the embassy*
Velika Britanija: Velike Britanije	*Great Britain: of Great Britain*

David Jaz sem David. Tudi jaz sem Anglež. V Sloveniji sem že pet let. Stanujem v Ljubljani. Moja žena je Slovenka. Razumem skoraj vse ampak govorim slabo.

tudi	*also*
že pet let	*for five years already*
stanujem	*I live*
Ljubljana: v Ljubljani	*Ljubljana: in Ljubljana*
moja žena	*my wife*
skoraj	*almost*
vse	*everything*
slabo	*badly*

Did you understand?

Answer the following questions in Slovene.

a What is Tanja's profession?
b What is Caroline doing in Slovenia?
c What is Klaus's profession and where does he work?
d For how long has Susan been in Slovenia?
e How competent is David's knowledge of the Slovene language?

Did you know?

1 Countries and inhabitants

Slovene words for most other countries of the world are similar to the English names and are easily recognizable. Here are some countries where English is spoken: **Kanada, Amerika, Avstralija, Nova Zelandija, Irska.**

ZDA (Združene Države Amerike)   *USA*

Two European countries might be challenging as the Slovene names are not as easy to recognize:

Nemčija	*Germany*
Madžarska	*Hungary*

A geography test

Here are the Slovene names of some European countries. Write the numbers of the countries in the map.

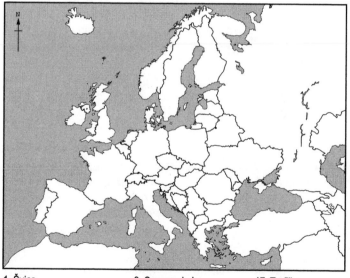

1 Švica	9 Severna Irska	17 Turčija
2 Italija	10 Belgija	18 Grčija
3 Portugalska	11 Češka	19 Švedska
4 Španija	12 Slovaška	20 Nizozemska
5 Avstrija	13 Poljska	21 Danska
6 Francija	14 Madžarska	22 Finska
7 Slovenija	15 Romunija	23 Nemčija
8 Velika Britanija	16 Bolgarija	24 Norveška

Countries and inhabitants of countries are spelt with a capital letter. Languages are spelt with a small letter in Slovene.

There are different forms for a woman and for a man of a partiuclar country. Look at the table below:

Country	Nationality		Language	One speaks
	Man	Woman		
Slovenija	Slovenec	Sloven**ka**	slovenščina	slovensko
Avstrija	Avstrijec	Avstrij**ka**	nemščina	nemško
Italija	Italijan	Italijan**ka**	italijanščina	italijansko
Nemčija	Nemec	Nem**ka**	nemščina	nemško
Madžarska	Madžar	Madžar**ka**	madžarščina	madžarsko
Francija	Francoz	Francoz**inja**	francoščina	francosko
Rusija	Rus	Rus**inja**	ruščina	rusko
Švedska	Šved	Šved**inja**	švedščina	švedsko
Turčija	Turek	Turk**inja**	turščina	turško
Anglija	Anglež	Anglež**inja**	angleščina	angleško

When a particular language, for example, **slovenščina**, is used as a subject, you say:

Slovenščina je težek jezik. *Slovene is a difficult language.*
Italijanščina je romanski jezik. *Italian is a romance language.*

težek	*difficult*
jezik	*language* (lit. *tongue*)
romanski	*romance*

When you want to say that you speak or understand a particular language you use the adverb, for example:

Razumem malo slovensko. *I understand a little Slovene.*

Govorim angleško. *I speak English.*

You may see some adverbs formed with a little word **po** in front, as in:

Kako se to reče po slovensko? *How do you say this in Slovene?*

Povej mi po angleško. *Tell me in English.*

2 The Slovene 'dual' form

In most languages singular and plural are used to indicate number. Slovene, however, has an additional 'dual' number, which is used when referring to two of anything. This dual number existed in many languages at one stage in their development, but has been lost; in Slovene, though, it has remained, and it is an integral part of both written and spoken language.

It might be useful to memorize the personal pronouns and the dual forms of the verb *to be*:

midva	*we two*	**midva sva**	*we two are*
vidva	*you two*	**vidva sta**	*you two are*
onadva	*they two*	**onadva sta**	*they two are*

Because of the dual form Slovene has a larger number of grammatical structures than some other languages. In this book we will not deal with the dual forms in detail. You will, from time to time, be reminded of dual so that you will not be taken aback if some of these forms come up in particular situations.

3 Poklic *(Profession)*

Words referring to occupations also have a masculine and feminine form. Look at the following examples:

	Man	**Woman**
student	študent	študentka
teacher	učitelj	učiteljica
assistant	asistent	asistentka
cook	kuhar	kuharica
shop assistant	prodajalec	prodajalka
accountant	računovodja	računovodkinja
doctor	zdravnik	zdravnica
singer	pevec	pevka
actor/actress	igralec	igralka

When you want to ask someone what they do for a living, you use the phrase:

Kaj si/ste po poklicu? *What do you do for a living?*

4 Slovene is a highly inflected language

The form of words in a sentence changes in Slovene according to the requirements of meaning and grammar. The term used for these changes is *inflexion* and because words change a great deal in Slovene, Slovene is regarded as a *highly inflected* language. Most of these changes apply to the endings of words. Don't worry at this stage if you don't know why a word has one ending in one sentence and a different ending in another. You will gradually learn when particular endings apply.

5 Article ('a', 'the')

You may have already noticed that you do not use an article (*a, an, the*) in Slovene when saying that you are of a particular nationality, or when talking about occupations. Articles are not used in Slovene. If this seems a problem, you will be reassured in the course of this book that Slovene manages very well without them!

▶ 6 Numbers 1–10

1	ena	6	šest
2	dva	7	sedem
3	tri	8	osem
4	štiri	9	devet
5	pet	10	deset

7 Verbs: Present tense

Verbs are words which express an action, such as *do, happen, say,* etc. The infinitive is that part of a verb which in English is preceded by 'to', for example, *to see, to go.* In Slovene infinitives are not preceded by anything corresponding to the English 'to' but usually end in -*ti* and sometimes in -*či*, e.g. **imeti** (*to have*), **teči** (*to run*).

In English only the third person singular (*he, she, it*) differs from all other forms of the verb, i.e. *he speaks* as opposed to *he speak.* In Slovene this is not the case. Each person has a different ending. The purpose of these endings is to make it clear who you are talking to or about. In other words, a verb must agree with the subject of the sentence in person and in number.

When we change the endings of a verb, we are *conjugating* the verb. There are rules as to how you formulate these endings.

This is the basic core of the verb, a form which is called the *stem*, onto which appropriate endings are added. This should help you to form all the other forms.

In Slovene there are three basic groups of verbs. An example of each is given below:

The verb **imeti** falls into *verbs of 'a' conjugation* because the stem of the verb ends in –a, the verb **razumeti** falls into *verbs of 'e' conjugation* because the stem ends in –e and the verb **govoriti** falls into *verbs of 'i' conjugation* because the stem ends in –i.

imeti *(to have)*	**razumeti** *(to understand)*	**govoriti** *(to speak)*
jaz im**am**	razum**em**	govor**im**
ti im**aš**	razum**eš**	govor**iš**
on im**a**	razum**e**	govor**i**
ona im**a**	razum**e**	govor**i**
ono im**a**	razum**e**	govor**i**
mi im**amo**	razum**emo**	govor**imo**
vi im**ate**	razum**ete**	govor**ite**
oni im**ajo**	razum**ejo**	govor**ijo**

It is not possible to know from the infinitive into which group a particular verb will fall. The verb **imeti**, for example, would logically fall into the 'e' group since there is an 'e' in the infinitive, but this is not the case. It is therefore important that you learn the third peron singular **on, ona, ono,** *he, she, it* (which is the stem of the verb), and add on the endings appropriate for other persons.

There are two additional groups of verbs. They are *verbs of 'ne' conjugation* (see the example **začeti** below) and *verbs of 'je' conjugation* (see the example **stanovati** below). Again, this means that their stem form ends in -ne or -je.

začeti *(to begin)*	**stanovati** *(to live)*
jaz zač**nem**	stau**jem**
ti zač**neš**	stanu**ješ**
on zač**ne**	stanu**je**
ona zač**ne**	stanu**je**
ono zač**ne**	stanu**je**
mi zač**nemo**	stanu**jemo**
vi zač**nete**	stanu**jete**
oni zač**nejo**	stanu**jejo**

The form of a verb which shows the *time* of an action is called *tense*. There are two present tenses in English (present simple, e.g. *I live*; and present continuous, e.g. *I am living*), but only one in Slovene, so that both these examples would be translated as **stanujem**.

8 Asking questions

You can ask a question in different ways in Slovene:

- by reversing the word order
- with the help of the question indicator **ali** (which can be omitted)
- by the intonation of your voice
- with the help of question words, such as *who? why? where?*

kje?	*where?*	**kdo?**	*who?*
kako?	*how?*	**kaj?**	*what?*
zakaj?	*why?*		

Look at the statements below, and the different ways of asking questions:

1 **Sara je v Sloveniji.**   *Sara is in Slovenia.*
  Je Sara v Sloveniji?   *Is Sara in Slovenia?*
  (Ali) je Sara v Sloveniji?   *Is Sara in Slovenia?*
  Sara je v Sloveniji?   *Sara is in Slovenia?*
  Kje je Sara?   *Where is Sara?*

2 **Govorijo dobro slovensko.**   *They speak Slovene well.*
  Ali govorijo dobro slovensko? *Do they speak Slovene well?*
  Govorijo dobro slovensko?   *They speak Slovene well?*
  Kako govorijo slovensko?   *How do they speak Slovene?*

9 How to make negative statements

When you want to negate something you simply put **ne** in front of a verb, for example:

Ne razumem slovensko.   *I don't understand Slovene.*
On ne govori špansko.   *He doesn't speak Spanish.*
Ne stanujemo v Ljubljani.   *We don't live in Ljubljana.*

The verb **biti**, as you saw in Unit 1, is an exception. The verb **imeti**, too, is slightly irregular and is negated by putting **n** in front of it, for example:

Nimam denarja.	I don't have any money.
Nimamo mleka.	We don't have any milk.

Remember!

How to

- ask if someone speaks a language, and reply:

Oprostite, ali govorite/ razumete ...?	Excuse me, do you speak/ understand ...?
Ja, govorim/razumem ...	Yes, I speak/understand ...
Ne, ne govorim/ne razumem ...	No, I don't speak/ understand ...

- ask where someone is from and where they live, and reply:

Od kod prihajate?	Where are you from?
Iz ... sem.	I'm from ...
Kje stanujete?	Where do you live?
Stanujem v ...	I live in ...

- ask someone what they do for a living, and reply:

Kaj si/ste po poklicu?	What do you do for a living?
Po poklicu sem ...	I am ...

- ask someone to speak slowly or to repeat what they said:

Govorite počasi, prosim!	Speak slowly, please!
Ponovite, prosim!	Repeat, please!

Exercises

1 Complete the following statements:

   a Sonja — slovensko. (*speaks*)
   b Tomaž ne — angleško. (*understands*)
   c Tanja — v Ljubljani. (*lives*)
   d Tanja — po poklicu učiteljica. (*is*)
   e Susan — dva sina. (*has*).
   f Klaus — na banki. (*works*)

2 You have just met a Slovene. Ask him the following questions:

   a   where he is from
   b   if he speaks English
   c   what he does for a living
   d   where he lives

3 Here are the names of some people competing in an international sports event. Can you tell from the towns they come from, what nationality they are?

   a   Janet: London
   b   Christin: Vienna
   c   Boris: Moscow
   d   Jean-Paul: Paris
   e   Henry: Manchester
   f   Johan: Berlin

4 Here are some statements. How would you contradict them?

   a   Delam na banki.
   b   Nataša stanuje v Berlinu.
   c   Moja mama govori dobro slovensko.
   d   Razumem francosko.
   e   Mitja je po poklicu kuhar.

5 **Križanka** *(Crossword)*

   a   doctor (male)
   b   language
   c   family
   d   shop assistant (male)
   e   actress
   f   singer (female)
   g   bank
   h   teacher (male)
   i   why
   j   where

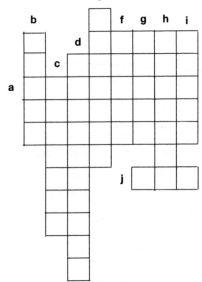

6 There are 14 countries in this wordsearch. Can you spot them?

A	L	B	A	N	I	J	A	K	I	C
M	A	D	Ž	A	R	S	K	A	T	M
F	R	A	N	C	I	J	A	I	A	K
I	F	I	N	S	K	A	N	N	L	A
R	F	Š	V	I	C	A	G	D	I	N
S	A	V	S	T	R	A	L	I	J	A
K	R	U	S	I	J	A	I	J	A	D
A	E	N	E	M	Č	I	J	A	T	A
R	O	M	U	N	I	J	A	S	L	V

7 Answer the questions below in Slovene, using the information from Duncan's introduction.

Ime mi je Duncan. Škot sem. Po poklicu sem kuhar. Delam v hotelu. V Sloveniji sem na dopustu.

a What nationality is Duncan?
b What is his occupation?
c Where does he work?

▶ **8** Introduce yourself to a group of Slovenes by saying what your name is, what nationality you are, what your profession is and where you work.

9 Tell a Slovene that you understand a bit of Slovene but that you don't speak very well.

▶ **10** Complete this conversation between two men in a bar by filling in the part of Vlado.

Vlado *(Ask Tim whether he lives in Ljubljana?)*
Tim Ne, v Ljubljani sem na izletu *(on a trip).*
Vlado *(Ask him where he is from)*
Tim Anglež sem.
Vlado *(Say, 'you speak Slovene well'.)*
Tim Hvala. Ali vi govorite angleško?
Vlado *(Say, 'I understand a lot but I speak badly'.)*

11 How good is your geography of Europe?

In the geography test at the beginning of this unit you spotted the countries of Europe. Slovene names for the capitals of those countries are listed below. Write down the country of which each city is the capital.

Note. *Like the names of the countries, the names of most capitals are easily recognizable, apart from* **Dunaj** (Vienna).

Lizbona	Ankara
Ljubljana	London
Rim	Praga
Dunaj	Pariz
Madrid	Budimpešta
Ženeva	Dublin
Oslo	Belfast
Bruselj	Bratislava
Varšava	Bukarešta
Sofija	Atene
Štokholm	Hag
Kopenhagen	Helsinki
Berlin	

▶ And something else...

Sara has enrolled in the Slovene course, but could not come the first day. In the next lesson, she speaks to Zmago, the assistant, over a cup of coffee.

Zmago	Si Američanka?
Sara	Ne, Angležinja sem. Iz Oxforda sem.
Zmago	Si prvič v Sloveniji?
Sara	Ja, že tri tedne sem tukaj.
Zmago	Kje stanuješ?
Sara	V Ljubljani, v centru. Pri eni družini.
Zmago	Dobro govoriš slovensko.
Sara	Hvala. Govorim malo, ampak razumem veliko. Slovenščina je težek jezik.
Zmago	Kako dolgo se že učiš slovensko?
Sara	Štiri leta.
Zmago	Pridna si! Jaz mislim, da je angleščina težek jezik.
Sara	Vsak jezik je po svoje težek.
Zmago	Ja, prav imaš!

iz Oxforda	*from Oxford*
prvič	*for the first time*
center: v centru	*centre: in the centre*
pri eni družini	*with a family*
učiti se	*to study*
vsak po svoje	*each in its own way*
prav imaš	*you're right*

03

prijeten konec tedna!

have a good weekend!

In this unit you will learn
- how to make enquiries about travelling
- how to use words for different means of travel
- how to purchase tickets and make reservations for different means of travel
- how to use more time expressions
- how to ask how much things cost
- how to deal with various means of payment
- how to count from 11 upwards

▶ Dialogues

Na železniški postaji *(At the station)*

A young tourist has arranged to see a friend who lives in Maribor, the second largest town in Slovenia. He goes to the ticket office in the railway station **železniška blagajna** to get a ticket.

Turist	Oprostite, koliko stane vozovnica do Maribora?
X	Enosmerna ali povratna?
Turist	Povratna, prosim.
X	Kdaj potujete?
Turist	V petek.
X	In kdaj pridete nazaj?
Turist	V nedeljo. Mimogrede, ali imam s študentsko izkaznico popust?
X	Samo trenutek, prosim.

blagajna	*cash desk*
železniška blagajna	*ticket office*
železniška postaja	*railway station*
(na železniški postaji)	*(at the railway station)*
Koliko stane?	*How much is it?*
vozovnica	*ticket*
do Maribora	*to Maribor*
enosmerna vozovnica	*one-way ticket*
povratna vozovnica	*return ticket*
Kdaj potujete?	*When are you travelling?*
v petek	*on Friday*
Kdaj pridete nazaj?	*When are you coming back?*
v nedeljo	*on Sunday*
mimogrede	*by the way*
študentska izkaznica	*student card*
(s študentsko izkaznico)	*(with a student card)*
popust	*discount*

▶ Mark, who lives in Slovenia, telephones an airline and books a ticket for a flight to London. Gospod Dolinšek answers the telephone.

Gospod Dolinšek	Prosim?
Mark	Dober dan. Rad bi rezerviral letalsko karto za London. Ali imate še prosta mesta?

Gospod Dolinšek	Ja, seveda. Kdaj pa potujete?
Mark	Naslednji torek, prosim.
Gospod Dolinšek	Samo trenutek, prosim. Žal mi je, gospod, ampak za naslednji torek je že vse rezervirano. V sredo in v četrtek so še prosta mesta.
Mark	In kdaj so poleti ob sredah?
Gospod Dolinšek	Zjutraj in zvečer. Tako kot vsak drugi dan.
Mark	Najlepša hvala za enkrat, gospod. Malo moram premisliti.
Gospod Dolinšek	Če želite potovati naslednji teden, vam priporočam, da se kmalu odločite in rezervirate karto.

Rad bi rezerviral ... (m) **Rada bi rezervirala ...** (f)	*I'd like to reserve*
letalska karta	*plane ticket*
prosta mesta	*free places*
kdaj (kdaj pa)	*when (and when)*
potovati	*to travel*
naslednji torek	*next Tuesday*
je že vse rezervirano	*is already all reserved*
v sredo in v četrtek	*on Wednesday and on Thursday*
poleti	*flights*
zjutraj/zvečer	*in the morning/in the evening*
tako kot	*like, just as*
vsak drugi dan	*every other day*
za enkrat	*for now, for the time being*
Malo moram premisliti	*I have to think about it a little*
če	*if*
želeti	*wish*
priporočati	*to recommend*
da	*that*
kmalu	*soon*
odločiti se	*to decide*

Did you understand?

a When does the tourist want to travel to Maribor?
b Does he want a single or a return ticket?
c When are the daily flights from Ljubljana to London?

Did you know?

1 Vikend (Weekend)

This is not a misspelling in Slovene, but the result of something that happens when words are borrowed from other languages. As you know, Slovene is very phonetic, and you pronounce the word 'weekend' **vikend**! It is a widely used word, and it has two meanings:

- it means, as in English, the days at the end of a week. The Slovene word to express this is **konec tedna** lit. 'end of the week.'
- It can refer to a little house which people have and where they spend their weekend.

You will be able to tell from the context of a conversation or a piece of writing which meaning is in question.

2 Adapted words

Vikend is only one of those adapted words widely used in Slovene. Although it has been 'Slovenized', it does retain the original, in this case English, meaning. There are a number of other words in Slovene which have come from other languages. They are spelt differently, but you will be able to recognize and understand them. Here are a few examples: **sendvič, turist, tvid** (fabric), **recepcija, inflacija**, etc.

3 Kdaj? (When?) – time expressions

Unlike in English, no preposition is needed when answering the question *when?* in Slovene (e.g. *in the morning, in the evening*, etc.). The word, however, changes slightly.

jutro	morning	zjutraj	in the morning
dopoldan	morning	dopoldne	in the morning
opoldan	midday	opoldne	at midday
popoldan	afternoon	popoldne	in the afternoon
dan	day	podnevi	by day
večer	evening	zvečer	in the evening
noč	night	ponoči	at night

▶4 Days of the week

The days of the week may seem difficult to remember at first, but one has to know them sooner or later. They are spelt with a small letter in Slovene (unless they occur at the beginning of a sentence). Look at the table below.

In the column next to the days are the abbreviations of the days.

Notice that after the preposition **v** (*on*) days ending in **-a** change to **-o**.

When something always happens on certain days, the preposition **ob** (*on*) is used. The days ending in **-a** get an additional **-h** ending, and the others drop the 'e' between the last two consonants and get an **-ih** ending. (These are *locative* endings – see Unit 11.)

ponedeljek	(po)	Monday	v ponedeljek	ob ponedeljkih
torek	(to)	Tuesday	v torek	ob torkih
sreda	(sre)	Wednesday	v sredo	ob sredah
četrtek	(če)	Thursday	v četrtek	ob četrtkih
petek	(pe)	Friday	v petek	ob petkih
sobota	(so)	Saturday	v soboto	ob sobotah
nedelja	(ne)	Sunday	v nedeljo	ob nedeljah

V petek popoldne sem doma.

I'm at home on Friday afternoon.

Ob sobotah dopoldne delam.

I work in the morning on Saturdays.

▶5 Months of the year

Like the days of the week, the months of the year are spelt with a small letter. They are very similar to the English words. To express '*in a particular month*' you don't need a preposition, but you change the ending.

januar	januar**ja**	*in January*
februar	februar**ja**	*in February*
marec	mar**ca**	*in March*
april	april**a**	*in April*
maj	maj**a**	*in May*
junij	juni**ja**	*in June*
julij	juli**ja**	*in July*
avgust	avgust**a**	*in August*
september	septemb**ra**	*in September*
oktober	oktob**ra**	*in October*
november	novemb**ra**	*in November*
december	decemb**ra**	*in December*

Kdaj greš v Slovenijo?	*When are you going to Slovenia?*
Avgusta.	*In August.*

6 Seasons

Like the months, **letni časi** (*the seasons*) simply change their endings when you want to say that somthing is happening in a particular season.

pomlad	*spring*	**spomladi**	*in spring*
poletje	*summer*	**poleti**	*in summer*
jesen	*fall, autumn*	**jeseni**	*in autumn*
zima	*winter*	**pozimi**	*in winter*

Here are a few examples:

Pomlad je prišla.	*Spring has arrived.*
Spomladi so dnevi daljši.	*In spring the days are longer.*
Zima je moj najljubši letni čas.	*Winter is my favourite season.*
Pozimi je mrzlo.	*In winter it is cold.*

▶ 7 Numbers

11–19		20–100		1,000–1 million	
11	enajst	20	dvajset	1,000	tisoč
12	dvanajst	30	trideset	10,000	deset tisoč
13	trinajst	40	štirideset	100,000	sto tisoč
14	štirinajst	50	petdeset	1,000,000	milijon
15	petnajst	60	šestdeset		
16	šestnajst	70	sedemdeset		
17	sedemnajst	80	osemdeset		
18	osemnajst	90	devetdeset		
19	devetnajst	100	sto		

To say a two-digit number you have to begin with the last number, e.g. to say 'thirty-three' you would say 'three-and-thirty' (**triintrideset**). Once you know the numbers from 1 to 9 and the numbers by groups of ten, they are easy to construct. They follow the pattern below:

21–29		51–59	
21	enaindvajset	51	enainpetdeset
22	dvaindvajset	52	dvainpetdeset
23	triindvajset	53	triinpetdeset
24	štiriindvajset	54	štiriinpetdeset
25	petindvajset	55	petinpetdeset
26	šestindvajset	56	šestinpetdeset
27	sedemindvajset	57	sedeminpetdeset
28	osemindvajset	58	oseminpetdeset
29	devetindvajset	59	devetinpetdeset

8 Nouns

Nouns are 'naming words', such as *book*, *tree*, *war*, *peace*, *Ljubljana*, *John*, etc. Slovene nouns are characterized by gender, case and number. There are:

- *three genders*: masculine, feminine and neuter
- *six cases*: nominative, genitive, dative, accusative, locative and instrumental
- *three numbers*: singular, dual and plural

Nouns (and numbers) are *declined*, which means that they change their form from one case to another, depending on their function in a given sentence.

You can recognize the gender of a noun by its ending.

- *Masculine* nouns end in a consonant:

      vlak   *train*
      prijatelj   *friend (male)*
      Anglež   *Englishman*

- *Feminine* nouns end in –a:

      hiša   *house*
      prijateljica *friend (female)*
      Slovenka   *Slovene woman*

There are nouns which do not follow these rules. The two seasons, **pomlad** and **jesen**, end in a consonant, and should therefore be masculine in gender. They are, however, feminine.

There are quite a few feminine nouns ending in a consonant. One of those nouns, which is feminine in most languages, is **ljubezen** (*love*).

- *Neuter* nouns end in –o or –e:

  mesto   *town, city*
  morje   *sea*
  drevo   *tree*

9 Around and about

To get around you will need to know the words for transport:

avtobus	*bus, coach*
vlak	*train*
letalo	*plane*
avto	*car*
peš	*on foot*
avtobusna postaja	*bus, coach station*
železniška postaja	*railway station*
letališče	*airport*

The *instrumental* case is used to express *by means of* something, literally *by* or *with* something. Look at the examples and the endings that these words take:

z avtobus**om**
z vlak**om**
z letal**om**
z avt**om**
s taksij**em**

10 Kako plačate? *(How will you pay?)*

Here are some words for dealing with payment. In the first columns, they are in the nominative case, the case in which words are listed in the dictionary. When you say that you pay by these means, they take instrumental endings.

kreditna kartica	*credit card*
s kreditn**o** kartic**o**	*by credit card*
ček	*cheque*
s ček**om**	*by cheque*
potovalni ček	*traveller's cheque*
s potovalni**m** ček**om**	*by traveller's cheque*
gotovina	*cash*
z gotovin**o**	*by cash*

The letters **s** and **z** are prepositions. They both mean *with*. Which you use depends on the first letter of the word they go with: use **s** before p, f, t, c, č, s, š, k, h. Otherwise, use **z**.

Remember!

How to

- ask how much something costs:

Koliko stane ...?	*How much is ...?*
Koliko stanejo ...?	*How much are ...?*
Koliko to stane?	*How much is this?*

- tell someone how are you paying:

s kreditno kartico	*by credit card*
s čekom	*by cheque*
s potovalnim čekom	*by traveller's cheque*
z gotovino	*by cash*

  (Remember the word for discount: **popust**.)

- ask when something is happening:

kdaj?	*when?*

Exercises

1 Which day of the week is missing in the box?

torek   nedelja   *četrtek*

ponedeljek   petek   sreda

2 What are the Slovene words for the days of the week?

3 What are two meanings of **vikend**?

4 Which number is missing from this sequence?
enainsedemdeset, dvainsedemdeset, triinsedemdeset, štiriinsedemdeset, šestinsedemdeset, sedeminsedemdeset.

5 You were told to come to collect your clothes from the dry cleaner **v četrtek popoldne**. When was that?

6 A shop assistant asks you, '**Kako plačate?**' Tell her '*by credit card*'.

7 You arrive at the arranged meeting and someone asks you how you got there. Tell him, *by car.*

8 Which is the odd word out? **pomlad, jesen, ljubezen, poletje, zima.**

9 A friend asks you when you are going on holiday next year. Tell her '*in February and in August*'.

10 Can you count backwards from 19 to 11?

11 Here are some nouns. What gender are they?

a	letalo	**e**	torek
b	letališče	**f**	nedelja
c	vlak	**g**	popust
d	avtobus	**h**	vozovnica

12 Did you understand all the words above?

▶ And something else ...

Mark decided to travel to London **v četrtek**. As he arrives at the hotel where he has booked a room a *receptionist*, **receptorka**, greets him.

Receptorka	Dober večer. Želite prosim?
Mark	Dober večer. Jaz sem Mark Nott. Imam rezervacijo za tri dni v hotelu.
Receptorka	Samo trenutek, prosim.
	(*She comes back.*)
	Ja, gospod Nott, vse je urejeno. Ali imate pri sebi kakšen osebni dokument? Potni list ali vozniško dovoljenje?
Mark	Ja, izvolite. Tukaj je moj potni list. Mimogrede, ali imam s študentsko izkaznico popust?
Receptorka	Na žalost ne. Številka vaše sobe je osemintrideset. Izvolite ključ. Dobrodošli v Sloveniji in prijeten konec tedna!
Mark	Hvala.

za tri dni	*for three days*
vse je urejeno	*everything is arranged*
imeti pri sebi	*to have on you*
kakšen	*some*
osebni dokument	*personal document*
potni list	*passport*
vozniško dovoljenje	*driving licence*
številka sobe	*room number*
ključ	*key*

04

na levo ali na desno?

left or right?

In this unit you will learn
- how to ask for and give basic directions
- how to use the imperative (command) form
- how to make negative statements
- how to express 'can' and 'must'

▶ Dialogues

Oprostite, kje je ...? *(Excuse me, where is ...?)*

A tourist in Ljubljana asks a local where one or two places are.

Turist	Oprostite, kje je Tromostovje?
Ljubljančan	Pojdite naravnost po tej glavni cesti in pri semaforju zavijte na levo. Ulica se imenuje Čopova ulica. Pojdite do konca te ulice in tam je Tromostovje.
Turist	Ali je daleč?
Ljubljančan	Ne, 10 minut hoje je.
Turist	Hvala.

pojdite	*go* (imperative for polite and plural)
naravnost	*straight on*
glavna cesta: po tej glavni cesti	*main road: on this main road*
semafor: pri semaforju	*traffic lights: at the traffic lights*
zavijte	*turn* (imperative for polite and plural)
ulica	*street*
se imenuje	*is called*
konec: do konca	*end: to the end*
te ulice	*of this street*
tam	*there*
daleč	*far*
10 minut hoje	*10 minutes' walk*

▶ Oprostite, ali veste mogoče ...? *(Excuse me, do you happen to know ...?)*

Turist	Oprostite, ali veste mogoče, kje je kakšna dobra gostilna?
Ljubljančan	Ob reki jih je veliko. Pojdite naravnost in ko pridete do Ljubljanice, zavijte na desno.
Turist	Hvala.

Ali veste mogoče ...?	*Do you happen to know ...?*
kakšna	*some*
dobra gostilna	*good pub*
reka: ob reki	*river: by the river*
jih je veliko	*there are many*
naravnost	*straight on*
ko	*when*
pridete	*you come* (plural and polite)
Ljubljanica	*river that flows through Ljubljana*
na desno	*to the right*

▶ Oprostite, ali lahko ...? *(Excuse me, can I ...?)*

Turist Oprostite, ali lahko tukaj parkiram?
Pešec Žal mi je, ne vem. Nisem iz Ljubljane.

ali lahko ...?	*can ...?*
tukaj	*here*
parkirati	*to park*
pešec	*pedestrian*
ne vem	*I don't know*
nisem iz	*I am not from*

Did you understand?

a Which road is the tourist supposed to follow to get to Tromostovje?
b Where are there a lot of pubs in Ljubljana?
c Which river flows through Ljubljana?

Did you know?

1 Ljubljana

Ljubljana is the capital of Slovenia, with some 330,000 inhabitants.

2 Ljubljančan – Ljubljančanka

You already know that there is a different form for a woman who comes from a particular country and for a man. There is also a different form for men and women from particular towns, equivalent to the English *Londoner*, for example. In the case of the town Ljubljana, a *man* from Ljubljana is **Ljubljančan** and a *woman* is **Ljubljančanka**. The same goes for all other towns.

3 Adjectives

Adjectives are words which *describe* things and they, too, change endings according to the gender of the noun they describe:

- masculine adjectives end in a consonant
- feminine adjectives end in –**a**
- neuter adjectives end in –**o**
- The letter –**e**–, which appears in a lot of masculine adjectives between the final two consonants, disappears when you add –**a** for feminine and –**o** for neuter adjectives

Maculine	Feminine	Neuter
velik pes *large dog*	velik**a** torba *large bag*	velik**o** mesto *large town*
lep pulover *beautiful pullover*	lep**a** hiša *beautiful house*	lep**o** vreme *nice weather*
dober dan *good day*	dob**ra** večerja *good supper*	dob**ro** jutro *good morning*

4 Glavni – glavna – glavno (main)

The word **glava** means *head*. From this you get the adjective **glavni, –a, –o**, meaning *main*, as in, for example:

glavn**i** vhod	*main entrance*
glavn**a** cesta	*main road*
glavn**o** mesto	*capital city*

5 Kakšen – kakšna – kakšno? *(What? what kind of?)*

You will come across this question indicator in a variety of contexts. It can mean *what? what kind of?* and its different forms indicate the gender of the noun it goes with, for example:

Kakš**en** avto imaš? (m.)	*What car do you have?*
Kakš**no** je danes vreme? (n.)	*What's the weather like today?*
Kakš**na** je vaša telefonska številka?	*What is your telephone number?*

You might also encounter this word when it means *What a ...*, as in this example:

Kakšna lepa hiša!   *What a nice house!*

6 Possessive adjectives

Like all other adjectives, possessive adjectives change endings according to the gender of the noun. Look at the examples below.

Note. There are a number of new nouns given as examples. You are not expected to memorize them all, but they are all listed in the glossaries at the back.

	Masculine	Feminine	Neuter
my, mine	**moj** denar	**moja** torba	**moje** delo
your(s)	**tvoj** rojstni dan	**tvoja** obletnica	**tvoje** spričevalo
his	**njegov** svinčnik	**njegova** aktovka	**njegovo** pero
her	**njen** zvezek	**njena** beležka	**njeno** ravnilo
its	**njegov** dežnik	**njegova** denarnica	**njegovo** kolo
our(s)	**naš** kraj	**naša** ulica	**naše** mesto
your(s)	**vaš** stanovanjski blok	**vaša** hiša	**vaše** stanovanje
their(s)	**njihov** pes	**njihova** spalnica	**njihovo** okno

Adjectives modifying neuter nouns usually end in **–o**, but when the adjective stem ends in **–c, –č, –š, –z, –j** its neuter form ends in **–e**, as, for example:

tvoj*e* delo   naš*e* mesto
rdeč*e* vino   vaš*e* stanovanje
vroč*e* vreme

7 Negative statements

Verbs form their negative by putting **ne** in front of the verb, for example:

Infinitive		Positive	Negative
govoriti	*to speak*	jaz govorim	jaz **ne** govorim
vedeti	*to know*	jaz vem	jaz **ne** vem

There are three verbs which form their negative with a single word:

Infinitive		Positive	Negative
biti	*to be*	jaz sem	jaz **ni**sem
imeti	*to have*	jaz imam	jaz **ni**mam
hoteti	*to want*	jaz hočem	jaz **no**čem

8 'To go' and 'to come'

These are verbs one needs a lot. They are, unfortunately, irregular, and you have to learn them:

	iti *(to go)*	**priti** *(to come)*
jaz	grem	pridem
ti	greš	prideš
on ona } ono	gre	pride
mi	gremo	pridemo
vi	greste	pridete
oni	grejo	pridejo

9 'To walk'

In order to express *to walk*, *to go on foot*, you use the verb *to go* plus the adverb **peš**. The adverb **peš** never changes; you conjugate the verb to indicate who you are referring to, for example.

Kako prideš?	*How are you coming?*
Pridem peš.	*I'm walking.*
Ali greš peš v mesto?	*Are you going to town on foot?*
Ne, jaz nikoli ne grem peš!	*No, I never go on foot!*

10 Imperative (command form)

The imperative is the particular form of a verb which is used when telling someone what to do, or what not to do. It is sometimes called the 'command form', although it does not necessarily mean that you are giving a command. It is used in written instructions, such as recipes, DIY books, car service handbooks, manuals, etc.

It is also used to give directions to someone. This is why the verbs in the dialogues in this unit were in the imperative form.

In Slovene there are three forms for the imperative: one corresponds to the familiar, one to the polite, and one to the 'we' form – this would correspond to the English 'Lets do something', i.e. when you mean that 'we should all do' something. The verbs will take the following endings:

	Verbs of 'a' conjugation	Verbs of 'e' conjugation	Verbs of 'i' conjugation
you (singular)	**-aj**	**-i**	**-i**
you (plural)	**-ajte**	**-ite**	**-ite**
'we' form	**-ajmo**	**-imo**	**-imo**

Here are some examples of the imperative in use:

Vozi previdno!	*Drive carefully!*
Ne kadite, prosim!	*Do not smoke, please!*
Ne delaj se neumnega!	*Don't play the fool!*

As you would expect, there are some irregular forms, which do not follow the pattern above. Some commonly used irregular verbs in the imperative form are:

biti	**iti**	**imeti**
bodi!	pojdi!	imej!
bodite!	pojdite!	imejte!
bodimo!	pojdimo!	imejmo!

11 How to express *'can'*

To express *can* you need to use the adverb **lahko** and the verb in a form which will indicate who you are talking about, for example:

Ali grem lahko peš?	*Can I walk?*
Tukaj lahko kadiš.	*You can smoke here.*

This only works for positive statements or for questions. You will see later on how to express 'cannot'.

12 How to express *'must'*

The word for *must* is **morati**. It is a verb and is conjugated, like all other verbs. The forms are as follows:

mor**am**	*I must*
mora**š**	*you must* (sg.)
mor**a**	*he, she, it must*
mor**amo**	*we must*
mor**ate**	*you must* (pl.)
mor**ajo**	*they must*

When you want to say that someone must do something you use **morati** and the *infinitive form of the verb* which states what must be done, for example:

Moram telefonirati.	*I must telephone.*
Ali moraš kupiti še kaj?	*Do you have to buy anything else?*
Moramo iti v mesto.	*We must go to town.*

As with the verb *can*, this works for positive statements and questions. You will see later on how to express the negative form of this verb.

▶ Remember!

How to

- ask for directions:

  Oprostite, kje je ...?   *Excuse me, where is ...?*
  Ali veste mogoče, kje je ...?   *Do you happen to know where ... is?*

- tell someone that you don't know:

  Žal mi je, ne vem.   *I'm sorry, I don't know*

- say where something is:

  na levo   *on the left*

  na desno   *on the right*

  naravnost   *straight on*

- say 'can':

  lahko + the verb in a correct personal form

- say 'must':

  Morati in a correct personal form + the infinitive of the verb telling what must be done

Exercises

▶ **1a** Someone stops you on the road and asks you where the nearest post office is. Tell him to go straight on and turn right at the traffic lights.

   b He asks you: 'Ali je daleč?' What does he want to know?

   c Tell him that it is five minutes' walk.

▶ **2** You are stopped in the centre of Ljubljana and asked: 'Ali veste mogoče, kje je kakšna dobra restavracija?'

Say to the person who stopped you: 'I'm sorry, I don't know. I'm not from Ljubljana.'

▶ 3 You are on a train going to visit another town in Slovenia. A woman sitting opposite you says something to you rather fast. Say to her: 'I'm sorry, I don't speak Slovene well.'

She then asks you more slowly: 'Ste na dopustu?'

Tell her: 'No, I'm not on holiday. I'm here on business. I work at a bank.'

She is quite keen to talk to you, and asks: 'Ali vam je všeč v Sloveniji?'

Answer by saying: 'Yes, I like it.'

4 You have been given your diary for the week ahead. Tell your friend what you must do on each day. The first example has been done for you.

a PO pojdi v banko. — **V ponedeljek moram iti v banko.**
b TO pojdi na sestanek ob desetih dopoldne.
c SR pojdi na pošto.
d ČE kupi karte za v kino.
e PE telefoniraj Sonji.

5 You arrive at a meeting on a day there is a public transport strike and your colleague asks you: 'Kako si prišel?'
Tell her: 'I came on foot.'

6 Your office operates a non smoking policy. A visitor is just about to light a cigarette and aks you: 'Can I smoke here?'
How did he say that?
Tell him: 'We don't smoke here.'

7 Since people know that you are used to driving on the left and that driving on the right is a change for you, they often tell you: 'Drive carefully!' How do they say that in Slovene?

8 Fill in the correct form of possessive adjective in Slovene as indicated in brackets.

a — denar (*his*)
b — dežnik (*her*)
c — knjiga (*my*)
d — hiša (*their*)
e — denarnica (*her*)
f — stanovanje (*our*)
g — delo (*your*)
h — avto (*their*)

▶ And something else …

Vodič, a tourist guide, is taking a group of people around Ljubljana. When they stop in the centre of town, he tells them the following:

"Smo v središču mesta, na Trgu republike, ki je gospodarsko, politično in kulturno središče Ljubljane. Peš gremo lahko do Tromostovja. Reka, ki teče skozi Ljubljano, se imenuje Ljubljanica. Na tej strani je novi del mesta, na drugi strani reke pa je staro mesto. Nad njim vidite Ljubljanski grad. Del središča mesta je zaprt za promet, to pomeni, da je namenjen peščem. Tukaj je veliko trgovin in kavarn. Po kosilu gremo lahko peš do nekaj kulturnih ustanov. Med njimi so: Opera, Drama, Moderna Galerija, Narodni Muzej in Ljubljanska Univerza."

v središču mesta	*in the centre of town*
gospodarsko, politično in	*economic, political and cultural*
kulturno središče Ljubljane	*centre of Ljubljana*
ki teče	*which runs*
skozi Ljubljano	*through Ljubljana*
se imenuje	*is called*
na tej strani	*on this side*
novi del mesta	*new town*
na drugi strani	*on the other side*
staro mesto	*old town*
nad njim	*above it*
Ljubljanski grad	*Ljubljana castle*
del središča mesta	*a part of the centre of town*
je zaprt za promet	*is closed to traffic*
je namenjen peščem	*is intended for pedestrians*
veliko trgovin in kavarn	*a lot of shops and cafés*
po kosilu	*after lunch*
nekaj kulturnih ustanov	*a few cultural institutions*
med njimi so	*amongst them are*
Drama	*theatre*
Moderna Galerija	*Modern Gallery*
Narodni Muzej	*National Museum*
Ljubljanska Univerza	*Ljubljana University*

05

imam novo telefonsko številko!

I have a new telephone number!

In this unit you will learn
- how to handle transactions at the post office and the bank
- how to make arrangements on the telephone
- how to use the ordinal numbers (i.e. first, second, etc.)
- how to use words for colours
- how to use adverbs
- how to use the accusative case

▶ Dialogues

Po telefonu *(Over the telephone)*

Pamela, who is on holiday in Slovenia, wants to telephone home. She rings the post office, **pošta,** to find out what the code number for England is.

Poštni uslužbenec	Prosim?
Pamela	Dober dan, je to pošta?
Poštni uslužbenec	Ja, to je glavna pošta. Kaj lahko storim za vas?
Pamela	Povejte mi prosim, kakšna je predklicna številka za Anglijo.
Poštni uslužbenec	0044.
Pamela	Najlepša hvala, na svidenje.

Kaj lahko storim za vas?	*What can I do for you?*
Povejte mi prosim …	*Tell me, please …*
predklicna številka	*code number*

Po opravkih v mestu *(Things to be seen to in town)*

Pamela has to change some money and asks a passer-by where the nearest bank is.

Pamela	Oprostite, kje je najbližja banka?
Pešec	Ali vidite tisti poštni nabiralnik? Rumen je. Tam zavijte na levo in druga ali tretja stavba na tisti ulici je banka.
Pamela	Hvala.

najbližji (-a, -e)	*the nearest*
Ali vidite tisti …?	*Do you see that …?*
poštni nabiralnik	*post box*
rumen	*yellow*
druga ali tretja stavba	*second or third building*
ulica: na tisti ulici	*street: on that street*

▶ Na banki *(At the bank)*

Pamela	Dober dan. Rada bi zamenjala denar, 100 angleških funtov.
Bančni uradnik	Ali imate pri sebi potni list?
Pamela	Ne, vozniško dovoljenje imam. Izvolite.
Bančni uradnik	Ali imate morda kakšen dokument, ki ima vašo

	sliko?
Pamela	Mojo staro študentsko izkaznico imam.
Bančni uradnik	Samo trenutek, posvetovati se moram z mojim sodelavcem.

bančni uradnik	*bank clerk*
rad (-a) bi ...	*I'd like to ...*
zamenjal (-a) denar	*change some money*
x angleških funtov	*x English pounds*
pri sebi	*on you*
potni list	*passport*
vozniško dovoljenje	*driving licence*
morda	*perhaps*
ki	*which*
vašo sliko	*your photograph*
star (-a, -o)	*old*
posvetovati se	*consult*
sodelavec: z mojim sodelavcem	*colleague: with my colleague*

▶ Koliko je ura? *(What is the time?)*

Worried that she might miss her next appointment, Pamela asked a woman in the bank what time it was.

Pamela	Oprostite, koliko je ura?
Gospa	Ura je točno ena.

Ura je ...	*The time is ...*
točno	*exactly*

Did you understand?

a What is the code number for England from Slovenia?
b Do you remember what the word for a post box is?
c What sort of document does the bank official want to see?

▶ Did you know?

1 Po telefonu *(Over the telephone)*

The commonest way of answering the telephone is by saying **prosim?** You can also simply state the telephone number, or the name of the family whose telephone it is. If you are calling an organization, the telephonist will usually say the name of that organization. You can start a telephone conversation by greeting the person who answers the telephone, introducing yourself and asking for the person you would like to talk to, for example:

Dobro jutro, Janez pri telefonu.	*Good morning, Janez on the phone.*
Je Bojan tam?	*Is Bojan there?*

You can get a number of answers as a reply; here are some examples:

Trenutek, prosim.	*Just a moment, please.*
Vežem.	*Putting you through.*
Zasedeno je.	*It's engaged.*
Želite počakati?	*Do you wish to hold?*

If you wish to make a telephone call, look for or ask for **telefonska govorilnica** or **telefonska kabina** (telephone box). If you need the telephone directory ask for **telefonski imenik**.

The popularity of mobile telephones in Slovenia is growing all the time. The word for a mobile phone is **mobilni telefon** or just **mobi**.

2 At a post office

Post offices in Slovenia provide you with a normal post office service. The post boxes are yellow. Here are some words and phrases which you will find useful:

Kje je pošta?	*Where is the post office?*
pismo	*letter*
razglednica	*postcard*
kuverta	*envelope*
znamka	*stamp*
priporočeno	*registered*

If you tell the post office clerk to which country you are sending something, he or she will tell you the price of the stamp. Here are some phrases you need when buying anything:

Koliko stane ...?	*How much is ...?*
Koliko stanejo ...?	*How much are ...?*
Koliko to stane?	*How much is this?*

3 At the bank

The Slovene currency is **tolar**. The international sign for it is SIT. However, do not be surprised if you hear people talking about **eurih** which will become the legal currency in January 2007. When Slovenia became independent, a number of new banks were established. Because of growing competition amongst them, they have now fallen in number.

You might be asked to prove your identity at the bank. Your passport **potni list**, is your best bet. Slovenes can prove their identity with a *driving licence*, **vozniško dovoljenje**, as well, since it has an endorsed photograph. There is also a special *identity card*, **osebna izkaznica**, once compulsory and now optional, which serves as proof of identity.

Useful phrases for transactions at a bank

Note: *Revise your numbers!*

Kje je menjalnica?	*Where is the bureau de change?*
Želel(a) bi zamenjati ...	*I'd like to change ...*
50 angleških funtov	*£50*
100 ameriških dolarjev	*$100*
300 eurov	*300EUR*
Kje lahko zamenjam potovalne čeke?	*Where can I change traveller's cheques?*
Kakšen je menjalni tečaj?	*What's the exchange rate?*

4 Kakšne barve je ...? *(What colour is ...?)*

All colours are adjectives, and have three endings. Most neuter forms for colours end in –o. If the masculine form ends in c, č s, z or j then the neuter form will end in –e.

Masculine	Feminine	Neuter	
črn	črna	črno	black
bel	bela	belo	white
rdeč	rdeča	rdeče	red
moder	modra	modro	blue
rumen	rumena	rumeno	yellow
zelen	zelena	zeleno	green
rjav	rjava	rjavo	brown
siv	siva	sivo	grey
oranžen	oranžna	oranžno	orange

Do you remember what colour **poštni nabiralnik** is? It is **rumen**. Because **nabiralnik** ends in **k** it is a masculine noun, and the colour modifying it is therefore also in a masculine form.

The words **svetlo** (*light*) and **temno** (*dark*) are adverbs and never change their ending. For example:

Moj avto je temno moder.	*My car is dark blue.*
Njena nova torba je svetlo rjava.	*Her new bag is light brown.*

5 Adverbs

Adverbs are words which in English usually end in –ly, for example, *nicely*, *badly*, etc. You have already learnt that adjectives describe nouns. Adverbs are usually used to give a more precise meaning to verbs, e.g. *She cooks badly*. 'To cook' is a verb and 'badly' is the adverb: it tells us how she cooks.

In Slovene, the nominative neuter form of adjectives is used as an adverb i.e. to describe verbs. For example:

Govorim slovensko.	*I speak Slovene.*
Vozi previdno!	*Drive carefully!*
Pogovarjajo se zelo glasno.	*They talk very loudly.*

6 Reflexive verbs

In this unit you have come across verbs which include a short word, **se**. You met the verbs **imenovati se** (*to be called*), **posvetovati se** (*to consult*) and **pogovarjati se** (*to converse*). The verbs followed by **se** are called *reflexive* verbs. You conjugate the verb, but **se** never changes, for example: **imemujem se, imenuješ se, imenujejo se**, etc. You will learn more about these verbs in units to come.

7 Prvi, drugi, tretji ... *(First, second, third ...)*

You already know numbers! Numbers like 1, 3, 75 are called *cardinal* numbers. Numbers like 1*st*, 3*rd*, 75*th* are called *ordinal* numbers. In Slovene, they are indicated by having a full stop after them. They are adjectives, and are formed as follows:

1. prvi, –a ,–o	11. enajsti, –a ,–o	21. enaindvajseti, –a ,–o
2. drugi, –a ,–o	12. dvanajsti, –a ,–o	22. dvaindvajseti, –a ,–o
3. tretji, –a ,–e	13. trinajsti, –a ,–o	23. triindvajseti, –a ,–o
4. četrti, –a ,–o	14. štirinajsti, –a ,–o	24. štiriindvajseti, –a ,–o
5. peti, –a ,–o	15. petnajsti, –a ,–o	25. petindvajseti, –a ,–o
6. šesti, –a ,–o	16. šestnajsti, –a ,–o	26. šestindvajseti, –a ,–o
7. sedmi, –a ,–o	17. sedemnajsti, –a ,–o	27. sedemindvajseti, –a ,–o
8. osmi, –a ,–o	18. osemnajsti, –a ,–o	28. osemindvajseti, –a ,–o
9. deveti, –a ,–o	19. devetnajsti, –a ,–o	29. devetindvajseti, –a ,–o
10. deseti, –a ,–o	20. dvajseti, –a ,–o	30. trideseti, –a ,–o

You have to learn the ordinal numbers from 1st to 4th by heart. Note also that numbers 7 and 8 drop the -e- when they become ordinal i.e.

7 sedem   7th sedmi   8 osem   8th osmi

For numbers from 9 onwards, add:

i for *masculine*, e.g.   enajsti mesec   *11th month*
a for *feminine*, e.g.   enajsta napaka   *11th mistake*
o for *neuter*, e.g.   enajsto leto   *11th year*

8 Cases

You have already learnt that Slovene is an inflected language, which means that noun and verb endings change according to their function in the sentence.

When we talk about cases, we are talking about nouns. There are six cases in the Slovene noun system, each with a particular purpose or function. You might have come across the term 'declension', or 'to decline': this means putting a noun into its different cases.

The six Slovene cases and their functions are explained in brief below:

- *Nominative*: used as a subject of the sentence
- *Genitive*: used as a possessive, in negatives, and as the object of certain prepositions

- *Dative*: used as indirect object, and as the object of certain prepositions
- *Accusative*: used as direct object, and as the object of certain prepositions
- *Locative*: used as the object of certain prepositions, most often to express the location of something
- *Instrumental*: used as the object of certain prepositions

You know that nouns can be *masculine*, *feminine* or *neuter* gender. All nouns can be declined in singular, dual and plural. In this book we will only cover singular and plural, which correspond to English.

9 The accusative case

The relationships between words in a sentence are conveyed by word order in English; in Slovene they are conveyed by case endings. If a noun is the *subject* of a verb – this means that it precedes the verb in English – then it is in the nominative case. If, however, a noun is the *object* of a verb – this means that it follows the verb in English – then it is in the accusative case.

Look at the following examples:

Nominative	Accusative
Moja študentska izkaznica je stara. *My student card is old.*	Imam **staro študentsko izkaznico**. *I have an old student card.*
Poštni nabiralnik je rumen. *The post box is yellow.*	Ali vidite tisti **poštni nabiralnik**? *Do you see that post box?*
To je **moj prijatelj Milan**. *This is my friend Milan.*	Ali poznaš **mojega prijatelja Milana**? *Do you know my friend Milan?*
To je **moje vozniško dovoljenje**. *This is my driving licence?*	Ali imate pri sebi **vozniško dovoljenje**? *Do you have your driving licence on you?*

In the first column, nouns and adjectives (words in bold) are the *subject* of the sentence, and are therefore in the *nominative case*. In the second column, these nouns are the *object* of the sentence and are in the *accusative case*. The endings of these nouns have changed. The basic rules for changing them are as follows:

- *Feminine nouns* ending in –a change their ending to –o. (In the first example above, **študentska izkaznica** changes to **študentsko izkaznico**)

- *Masculine nouns denoting non-living objects* do not change their endings. (In the second example above, **poštni nabiralnik** remains **poštni nabiralnik**)
- *Masculine nouns denoting living objects* change their ending to **–a**. (In the third example above, **prijatelj Milan** changes to **prijatelja Milana**)
- *Neuter nouns* do not change their endings. (In the fourth example above, **vozniško dovoljenje** remains **vozniško dovoljenje**)

10 Adjectives in the accusative case

Adjectives describing nouns also change their endings: **študentska** in the first example changes to **študentsko**. They follow the same rules as the nouns, except in the case of masculine nouns denoting living objects, where the adjective ends in **–ega** in the accusative case: **moj** changes to **mojega** in the third example.

11 Personal pronouns in the accusative case

Pronouns stand in place of nouns. Personal pronouns in English are *I, you, he, she, it, we, you* pl. and *they*. The system of case endings still exists in English for personal pronouns. Look at these examples:

I saw Mark today.	I saw *him* today.
I saw Sheila yesterday.	I saw *her* yesterday.

'*Him*' and '*her*' are personal pronouns standing in place of 'Mark' and 'Sheila'. You could not say 'I saw he and she today', because '*he*' and '*she*' are personal pronouns in the *nominative* case. In the sentences above 'he' and 'she' are the objects of the verb 'to see' and are in the *accusative* case.

In Slovene, each personal pronoun has six different forms, one for each case. Some of them happen to be the same. Personal pronouns in the nominative and accusative cases are:

Nominative	Accusative
jaz	mene / me
ti	tebe / te
on	njega / ga
ona	njo / jo
ono	njega / ga
mi	nas
vi	vas
oni	njih / jih

Some personal pronouns have a long and short form. You will gradually learn which one is more appropriate to use in particular situations.

In the section appendices at the end of the book there is a table showing personal pronouns in all cases. You can refer to this table when you need to check which personal pronoun you should use.

Remember!

How to

- introduce yourself on the phone and ask if someone is there:

... pri telefonu. Je ... tam?	... *on the phone.*
	Is ... there?

reply to an inquiry:

Samo trenutek, prosim.	*Just a moment, please.*
Vežem.	*Putting you through.*
Zasedeno je.	*It's engaged.*

- name basic items at a post office:

pismo	*letter*
razglednica	*postcard*
znamka	*stamp*

- deal with basic financial transations:

Kje je menjalnica?	*Where is the bureau de change?*
Želel(a) bi zamenjati ...	*I'd like to change ...*
Kakšen je menjalni tečaj?	*What's the exchange rate?*

Exercises

1 You are out and about and want to make a telephone call. What are you looking for?

2 Which is the odd word out and why? **rdeč, zelen, rumena, rjav, moder, bel**

▶ 3 You need to pop into a bank. How would you ask a passer-by where the nearest bank is?

▶ 4 You go to a bank. Go up to the counter and say that you would like to change £50.

5 Test your vocabulary! Which of these words would be out of place in a bank?

> denar
>
> **potovalni čeki**
>
> kreditna kartica
>
> menjalnica
>
> znamka
>
> 300 ameriških dolarjev
>
> *tolar*
>
> razglednica

6 You have an important document to send to someone. Which word would you use to ask the post office clerk to send it by registered post?

7 Fill in the missing Slovene words as indicated

   a — pulover (*light brown*)   d — poštni nabiralnik (*yellow*)
   b — vino (*white*)   e — avto (*dark blue*)
   c — vino (*red*)   f — kuverta (*white*)

8 Match the words on the left with their opposites on the right.

   bela   slabo
   nov   temno
   dobro   enosmerna
   povratna   črna
   svetlo   star

▶ 9 If someone asks you **Oprostite, kje lahko zamenjam
potovalne čeke?** What does he want to know?

10 Say the following dates aloud:

a 11. december
b 26. februar
c 31. avgust
d 7. april

11 Put the nouns in brackets into the accusative case to
complete the sentences.

a Kupiti moram eno (razglednica) in (znamka).
b Ali imaš pri sebi (študentska izkaznica)?
c Ali že poznaš (novi učitelj)?

And something else ...

Edward Clarke works for an English white goods company
which does business with the Slovene counterpart firm, Gorenje.
He telephones Janko Kos to arrange their annual meeting.

Telefonistka	Gorenje, prosim?
Edward	Dobro jutro, Edward Clarke pri telefonu. Je Janko Kos tam?
Telefonistka	Samo trenutek, vežem ... Halo?
Edward	Ja?
Telefonistka	Gospod Clarke, linija je trenutno zasedena. Ali želite počakati en trenutek?
Edward	Ja, prosim.

The telephonist did put Edward through to Janko Kos, but
Edward was not able to speak to him. He got Janko's answering
machine message, which said the following:

**Tukaj je Janko Kos na interni 462. Na žalost me trenutno ni v
pisarni. Prosim vas, da po znaku pustite sporočilo na telefonski
tajnici in ko se vrnem, vas pokličem nazaj. Hvala.**

interna (na interni)	direct line (on the direct line)
pisarna	office
Me trenutno ni v pisarni.	I'm not in the office at the moment.
prosim vas	lit. *I'm asking you*
da	*that*
znak: po znaku	tone: after the tone
pustiti	to leave
sporočilo	message
telefonska tajnica: na telefonski tajnici	answering machine (lit. *telephone secretary*): on the answering machine
ko	when
vrniti se	to come back, to return
poklicati	to call
nazaj	back

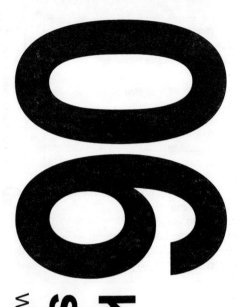

06
kdaj? ob sedmih zvečer
when? at 7 p.m.

In this unit you will learn
- how to ask for and tell the time
- how to say when something happens
- how to say that something happened in the past (using the past tense of the verb)
- how to write a note and a simple letter to someone
- how to say how many times something happened

▶ Dialogues

Sporočilo (A message)

Borut and Marko are studying at the same university and are good friends. Borut telephoned Marko yesterday, but could not reach him. He leaves him a note in his pigeon-hole:

> *Pozdravljen, Marko!*
>
> *Včeraj zvečer sem ti telefoniral, ampak ni te bilo doma. Kje si bil? Simon mi je dal dve vstopnici za predstavo v gledališču, ki je danes ob sedmih zvečer. Ali imaš čas danes zvečer? Telefoniraj mi popoldne in mi povej.*
>
> > *Lep pozdrav,*
> > *Borut*

sporočilo	*message*
včeraj	*yesterday*
večer: zvečer	*evening: in the evening*
sem ti telefoniral	*I telephoned you*
ampak	*but*
ni te bilo	*you were not*
doma	*at home*
si bil?	*were you?*
mi je dal	*gave me*
vstopnica: dve vstopnici	*ticket: two tickets*
predstava: za predstavo	*performance: for the performance*
gledališče: v gledališču	*theatre: in the theatre*
danes ob sedmih zvečer	*today at seven in the evening*
imaš čas	*you have time*
popoldne	*in the afternoon*
mi povej	*tell me*
Lep pozdrav	*Regards*

Note: *In Borut's note you saw quite a number of short words like* ti, te, mi. *These are personal pronouns in various cases. We will study them later on. If, however, you are using additional grammar books whilst studying and you already know something about these pronouns, an overall table of them shown in Appendix 3 at the back of the book might be of help to you.*

▶ Kje si bil včeraj zvečer? *(Where were you last night?)*

Marko telephoned Borut as soon as he got the message, as he was keen on that free outing in the evening. Borut, however, wanted to know what he had been up to the night before.

Marko	Živio, Borut, jaz sem. Ravnokar sem našel tvoje sporočilo.
Borut	Kje se bil včeraj zvečer? Trikrat ali štirikrat sem te poklical.
Marko	V kino sem šel. Z Ireno.
Borut	Ali imaš danes zvečer čas?
Marko	Ja, seveda. Že dolgo nisem bil v gledališču.
Borut	Jaz tudi ne. Letos sem bil samo enkrat.

ravnokar	*just*
sem našel	*found*
trikrat ali štirikrat	*three or four times*
Sem te poklical	*I called you*
kino: v kino	*cinema: to the cinema*
sem šel	*I went*
Irena: z Ireno	*Irena: with Irena*
že dolgo	*for a long time*
nisem bil	*I haven't been / I was not*
jaz tudi ne	*me neither*
leto: letos	*year: this year*
samo	*only*
enkrat	*once*

Did you understand?

a Who gave Borut the theatre tickets?
b When is the performance he is inviting Marko to?
c Where was Marko last night?

Did you know?

1 Enkrat, dvakrat, trikrat . . . *(Once, twice, three times . . .)*

When you want to say how many times something happens, you add the suffix **krat** onto the number, for example:

petkrat	5 times
desetkrat	10 times
dvaintridesetkrat	32 times

Here are a few other words which tell us how many times something happens, and which follow the same pattern, by adding **–krat** to the word.

velikokrat	many times
mnogokrat	many times
malokrat	few times

The following two words will also be of use:

nikoli	never
redko	rarely

2 Kdaj? *(Time expressions – When?)*

You are already familiar with a few words which tell us when something happened. You also know that you do not always need a preposition when you use a time expression, but simply add a prefix or a suffix to a word. Here are some time expressions. A few are for revision, and a few are new:

kdaj?	when?	zjutraj	in the morning
jutro	morning	dopoldne	in the morning
dopoldan	mid-morning	opoldne	at midday
opoldan	midday	popoldne	in the afternoon
popoldan	afternoon	zvečer	in the evening
večer	evening	ponoči	during the night
noč	night	podnevi	during the day
dan	day	letos	this year
leto	year	lani	last year

prejšnji, –a, –e	last
naslednji, –a, –e	next

The words **prejšnji** and **naslednji** are adjectives and change their adjectival endings depending on the noun, for example:

prejšnji mesec	*last month*
naslednja nedelja	*next Sunday*
naslednje leto	*next year*

3 Koliko je ura? *(What is the time?)*

The basic question for asking the time is: **Koliko je ura?** The answer to this question will usually be: **Ura je …** (*the time is …*).

Ura je tri. Ura je devet. Ura je dvanajst.

While in English you say 'it is three o'clock', you do not use the word 'o'clock' at the end of the sentence in Slovene.

The 24-hour clock is used on the radio and television, at railway stations and airports. In everyday speech people use the 12-hour clock; you can add the words **dopoldne, popoldne** or **ponoči**, if you think there might otherwise be a misunderstanding.

Numbers from five upwards are followed by the genitive case plural. (We will study this later on. For the time being this is only intended to tell you why you say, for example, **pet minut** or **deset ur**.)

ena ura	ena minuta	ena sekunda
dve uri	dve minuti	dve sekundi
tri ure	tri minute	tri sekunde
štiri ure	štiri minute	štiri sekunde
pet ur	pet minut	pet sekund

When you tell the time you use the hour and the minutes past the hour, for example:

Ura je pet in trideset minut. Ura je tri in petnajst minut. Ura je osem in petinštirideset minut. Ura je točno dve.

4 Ob šestih ali ob sedmih? *(At 6 or at 7?)*

The words 'case' and 'preposition' are already familiar to you. The short word '**ob**', which means '*at*' is a *preposition*, and it takes the *locative* case, about which we will talk later on.

Here are the numbers of the 12-hour clock in the locative case, which you should use if you want to say '*at* (say) *three o'clock*'. The prepositions **od** (*from*) and **do** (*until*) also take the locative case, and the same number endings are used with those. You would, for example, say:

Banka je odprta **od osmih do sedmih**. *The bank is open from 8 till 7.*

ob / od / do (*at / from / until*):			
1. enih	4. štirih	7. sedmih	10. desetih
2. dveh	5. petih	8. osmih	11. enajstih
3. treh	6. šestih	9. devetih	12. dvanajstih

5 Piši mi! *(Write to me!)*

If you are writing to a friend, it is common to start your message with:

Živio, Marko or **Pozdravljen**, Marko!

If you write to someone on more official terms, you start with:

Spoštovani gospod …! *or* **Spoštovana gospa …!**

You begin your letter with '*Dear …*' only if you are writing to someone with whom you are on affectionate terms:

Dragi …! *or* **Draga …!**

Notice that all appellations are followed by an exclamation mark!

To end your message, you would put a phrase like '**Lep pozdrav**' if *writing to a friend*, or '**S spoštovanjem**' which means '*with respect*', if you were writing to someone officially.

6 Past tense

You might be confused about the endings of the words you have seen so far but it's not that bad! Slovene makes up for it sometimes, and while there is no question that it takes a huge effort to master some things, tenses in Slovene are easy! First we shall study the past tense, which we use to express what happened in the past.

You have to know the present tense of the verb 'to be' in order to form the past tense. Together with the present tense of the verb 'to be' you use the *past participle*, which you get by:

- taking the infinitive form of the verb
- dropping the 'ti'
- and adding:
  - –l for *masculine*
  - –la for *feminine*
  - –lo for *neuter*
  - –li for *plural*

The past participle is used as an adjective, and so it has masculine, feminine and neuter endings. Let us see how this works in practice. Here are three infinitives:

telefonirati (*to telephone*); **videti** (*to see*); **povedati** (*to tell*)

To say: '*I telephoned*' you take the verb '*to be*' in the present tense (**sem**) and the verb **telefonirati**, from which you take off the –ti ending, and add –l (if you are a man). The phrase becomes: '**Sem telefoniral**'.

The same goes for **videti**: if you want to say '*you saw*', you say '**si videl**'.

'*They told*' would be '**so povedali**'.

Here are four verbs, conjugated in the past tense, as an example for you to follow:

	biti	telefonirati	videti	povedati
jaz	sem bil, –a	sem telefoniral, –a	sem videl, –a	sem povedal, –a
ti	si bil, –a	si telefoniral, –a	si videl, –a	si povedal, –a
on	je bil	je telefoniral	je videl	je povedal
ona	je bila	je telefonirala	je videla	je povedala
ono	je bilo	je telefoniralo	je videlo	je povedalo
mi	smo bili	smo telefonirali	smo videli	smo povedali
vi	ste bili	ste telefonirali	ste videli	ste povedali
oni	so bili	so telefonirali	so videli	so povedali

There is no exception to this rule, but there are exceptions as to how the past participle is formed. Verbs which do not form the past participle as explained above must be memorized. Here are some of them:

iti	(*to go*)	šel, šla, šlo, šli
priti	(*to come*)	prišel, prišla, prišlo, prišli
reči	(*to say*)	rekel, rekla, reklo, rekli
jesti	(*to eat*)	jedel, jedla, jedlo, jedli
piti	(*to drink*)	pil, pila, pilo, pili
najti	(*to find*)	našel, našla, našlo, našli

It might seem strange to you, but there is only one past tense in Slovene. '**Telefoniral sem**' can be translated as:

> *I telephoned*
> *I have telephoned*
> *I was telephoning*
> *I have been telephoning*

Note. *Only in written Slovene is the past perfect tense used (e.g.* I had telephoned), *but we will not deal with this tense.*

Negative statements in the past tense are formed simply by putting the verb '*to be*' in the negative form, for example:

Nisem še jedel.	*I haven't eaten yet.*
Ni bil doma.	*He wasn't at home.*
Nismo šli.	*We didn't go.*

7 Kakšno je danes vreme? *(What's the weather like today?)* Danes je lepo/slabo vreme. *(The weather is nice/bad today.)*

You might want to join in when the weather conversations start, so it is worth remembering the following two verbs:

deževati	*to rain*
snežiti	*to snow*

To say: '*it's raining*' or '*it's snowing*' you use the third person singular of these verbs, i.e.:

Dežuje.	*It's raining.*
Sneži.	*It's snowing.*

In the past tense you say:

Deževalo je.	*It was raining.*
Snežilo je.	*It was snowing.*

▶ Remember!

How to

- ask what time it is:

  Koliko je ura? *What time is it?*

- tell the time:

točno štiri	*exactly 4 o'clock*
štiri in petnajst minut	*4:15*
štiri in trideset minut	*4:30*
štiri in petinštirideset minut	*4:45*

- tell someone how many times something occurs:

  add **–krat** onto the number, e.g.

  štirikrat *four times*

- use verbs in the past tense:

  take the present tense of **biti,** the verb *'to be'* and a past participle, which you form by dropping the **–ti** ending from the verb and adding the adjectival ending **–l, –la, –lo** or **–li.**

  | **sem bil** | *I was* |
  | **si telefoniral** | *you telephoned* |

Exercises

1 A notice on the bank door says:

DELOVNE URE

po - pe	od 08 h / do 18 h
so	od 08 h / do 13 h
ne	zaprto

| **delovne ure** | *working hours* |

How would you tell someone what the bank opening hours are?

2 You are told that an event takes place **ob osmih zvečer.** When is that?

3 Which of these words is out of place? **zjutraj, dopoldne, popoldne, dan, ponoči, zvečer.**

4 You come back from a trip and are asked what the weather was like. How would you say: 'It was raining'?

5 **Koliko je ura?** Tell the time by both the 12-hour clock and the 24-hour clock.

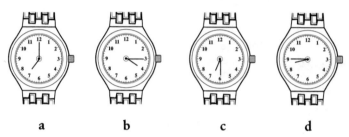

    a   **b**   **c**   **d**

6 Give answers to the questions below as suggested in brackets.

    a Kolikokrat si bil letos v gledališču? (*Three times.*)
    b Ali greš velikokrat v kino? (*No, rarely.*)
    c Ali si telefoniral Tamari? (*Yes, twice, but she wasn't at home.*)

▶ 7 A colleague at work asks you: '**Kdaj si imel sestanek?**' Tell him: 'Yesterday in the morning at 10 o'clock'.

8 Fill in the past tense of the verbs in the sentences below:

    a Včeraj (*I went*) v kino.
    b Domov (*I came*) ob enajstih zvečer.
    c (*I was*) zelo zaspan in utrujen.

9 A friend told you she was on holiday **prejšnji mesec.** When was that?

10 You are asked what the opening hours of a particular shop are. How would you say: 'from eight in the morning till seven in the evening'?

▶ And something else ...

On Saturday at 2:30 p.m. a tourist finds himself outside a post office door, which is closed. Wondering why, he approaches a passer-by.

Turist Oprostite, zakaj je zaprta pošta?

Pešec Sobota je. Ob sobotah je pošta odprta od osmih do enih. Sedaj je ura dve in trideset minut.

Turist Nisem vedel, da je pošta ob sobotah popoldne zaprta. Mislil sem, da pošta danes stavka.

Pešec Ne, ne, danes ne. Včasih že stavkajo, ampak danes dopoldne je bila pošta odprta. V soboto ob enih se vse zapre. Konec tedna je!

Turist Ja, razumem, ampak nisem vedel. Zapomniti si moram!

Pešec Ja, prijeten konec tedna!

Turist Hvala enako!

zakaj?	*why?*
je zaprt, –a, –o	*is closed*
je odprt, –a, –o	*is opened*
stavka	*strike*
stavkati	*to strike*
Se vse zapre.	*Everything closes.*
Zapomniti si moram.	*I must remember.*
Prijeten konec tedna.	*Have a good weekend.*
Hvala enako.	*The same to you.*

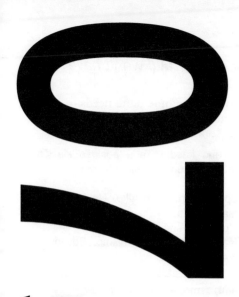

07

kar bo pa bo!

whatever will be will be!

In this unit you will learn
- how to say that you like something or like doing something
- how to talk about future events (using the future tense of the verb)
- how to ask questions about the future
- how to ask how someone is feeling and say how you feel
- how to use the dative case

▶ Dialogues

Ne bom imela dovolj prostora! *(I won't have enough space!)*

Sara has been in Slovenia over the summer, and needs to buy a few presents for her family and friends back home. She is talking about this to Irena, who has some suggestions.

Sara	Mami moram kupiti eno kaseta, rada posluša klasično glasbo. In sestri sem mislila kupiti nekaj na tržnici.
Irena	Dobra ideja!
Sara	In nujno moram kupiti še eno potovalko. Ne bom imela dovolj prostora za vsa ta darila.
Irena	Ne skrbi! Jaz ti bom posodila eno veliko torbo.
Sara	Sestri moram napisati še eno kratko pismo. Povedati ji moram, kdaj me mora priti počakat na letališče.

mama (mami)	*mother (for my mother)*
kaseta	*tape*
zgoščenka	*CD*
rada posluša	*she likes listening*
klasična glasba	*classical music*
sestra (sestri)	*sister (for my sister)*
nekaj	*something*
tržnica: na tržnici	*market: in the market*
dobra ideja	*good idea*
nujno	*urgently*
še eno	*another*
potovalka	*travelling bag*
ne bom imela	*I will not have*
dovolj	*enough*
prostor	*space*
vsa ta darila	*all those presents*
ne skrbi	*don't worry*
jaz ti bom posodila	*I will lend you*
eno veliko torbo	*one large bag*
napisati	*to write*
kratko pismo	*short letter*
povedati ji moram	*I must tell her*
priti počakat	*come to pick up*
na letališče	*to the airport*

▶V kavarni *(In a café)*

Before setting off to the shops, they stop at a café for a bite to eat.

Irena Imaš rada rižoto?
Sara Ja, zelo, ampak nisem lačna. Naročila bom samo en jabolčni zavitek.
Irena Jaz bom tudi samo nekaj malega. Tukaj vidim sirove palačinke. Boš kaj pila?
Sara Za enkrat ne. Kasneje bom kavo.
Irena Se slabo počutiš?
Sara Ne, ne, samo utrujena sem in malo zaskrbljena.

kavarna: v kavarni	*in a café*
Imaš rada rižoto?	*Do you like risotto?*
Nisem lačna.	*I'm not hungry.*
Naročila bom ...	*I will order ...*
jabolčni zavitek	*apple strudel*
Jaz bom tudi	*I will also.*
samo	*only*
nekaj malega	*something small*
sirove palačinke	*cheese pancakes*
Boš kaj pila?	*Will you have anything to drink?*
zaenkrat	*for the time being*
Kasneje bom kavo.	*I'll have a coffee later on.*
Se slabo počutiš?	*Are you feeling unwell?*
Utrujena sem.	*I'm tired.*
malo zaskrbljena	*a little worried*

Did you understand?

a What is Sara planning to buy for her mother and for her sister?
b What do they order in the café?

Did you know?

1 About Slovene food

The tendency in Slovenia is to follow international menus and, as elsewhere in Europe, fast food is becoming more and more popular due to changes in working hours and general lifestyle. So, you have trouble finding something typically Slovene. Some authentic Slovene dishes are **kraški pršut** (dried ham from the Karst region), **kranjske klobase** (sausages named after 'Kranjska' – the old name for Slovenia), **potica** (nut cake), **prekmurska gibanica** (cake with walnuts, apple and cheese filling). Due to the variety of geographical influences, Slovenes have adapted a number of German, Hungarian, Italian and Balkan dishes. In addition, dishes from those countries are very commonly on the menu in the respective border regions.

2 What do you like?

To say that you like something you use the verb **imeti** with the correct personal ending and the word **rad**, which is an adjective and therefore has the appropriate endings: rad (*m.*), rada (*f.*), radi (*pl.*).

For example:

Jaz imam rad kavo.
Marija ima rada čaj.
Vsi imamo radi črno kavo.

When you say what you like, the noun you are using will be in the accusative case, as the object of the sentence.

To say that you don't like something you simply use **imam** in its negative form, which is **nimam**, for example:

Nimam rad kave.

Note. *The noun* **kava**, *which was in the accusative case in the first example, has changed to* **kave**. *This is because when the negative is used nouns take the genitive ending. We will be looking into the genitive case in the next unit.*

To say that you *prefer* one thing to another you use the adverb **raje**, and to say that you like something *best* you use the adverb **najraje**, together with the verb **imeti**, for example:

Raje imam kavo.
Marija ima najraje čaj.
Vsi imamo najraje kavo.

Note. **Raje** *and* **najraje** *are not adjectives but adverbs, and so do not require different endings.*

3 What do you like doing?

To say that you like doing something you use the adjective **rad**, **rada**, **radi**, and the verb with the appropriate personal ending, for example:

Jaz rad pijem kavo.
Marija rada posluša klasično glasbo.
Vsi radi potujemo.

To say that you *prefer* doing something, you use the adverb **raje**; and to say that you like doing something *most* you use the adverb **najraje** and the appropriate form of verb, for example:

Raje pijem kavo.
Marija najraje posluša klasično glasbo.
Vsi najraje potujemo.

To say that you don't like doing something you put **ne** in front of the adjective **rad**, for example:

Jaz ne rad pijem kave.

4 How are you feeling?

The standard question to ask if you want to know how someone feels is:

Kako se počutiš (informal) or **Kako se počutite** (formal)? *How do you feel?*

The standard reply to this question is '**dobro**', if you feel well, and '**slabo**', if you don't feel well.

Here are some other words (all adjectives) which describe in more detail how you feel. They are all used with the verb '*to be*', which is placed at the end of the sentence rather than at the beginning, for example:

Zaspana sem.	*I'm sleepy.*
Utrujen je.	*He's tired.*
Zaskrbljeni so.	*They're worried.*

5 The dative case

The dative case is used in phrases like '*to say to*', '*to write to*', '*to give to*', '*to buy for*' someone. You have seen how Irena said that she had to buy something *for* her mother (*mam*i) and something for her sister (*sest*ri). 'Mother' and 'sister' were both in the dative case, and no preposition was used. Look at the following examples from the dialogue:

> Mami moram kupiti eno zgoščenko.
> Sestri moram napisati eno kratko pismo.

Dative case is most often used as an indirect object which indicates *for* or *to whom* something is done. In this example –

Irena piše sestri pismo.

– **pismo** is the *direct* object, and is in the *accusative* case; **sestri** is the *indirect* object, and is in the *dative* case.

The basic rules for the dative case are:

- *Feminine* nouns change their endings from **a** to **i**.
- *Masculine* and *neuter* nouns change their endings to **u**.

It is important to use the correct case ending. A wrong ending can change the meaning of a sentence, or make it difficult to understand what you actually mean. Look at these examples:

| Irena mora pisati sestri. | *Irena must write to her sister.* |
| Sestra mora pisati Ireni. | *Her sister must write to Irena.* |

These two sentences use the same words but have very different meanings. The relationships of the nouns to the verb indicate who must write to whom. In English the meaning is indicated by word order, and in Slovene, as you already know, it is indicated by case endings.

For personal pronouns in the dative case, see Appendix 3

6 Future tense

The future tense refers to actions which have yet to take place. In Slovene it is formed by using the *future tense* of the verb '*to be*' (**biti**) with the *past participle*. The future tense of **biti** has its own conjugation.

bom	*I will be*	bomo	*we will be*
boš	*you* (sg.) *will be*	boste	*you* (pl.) *will be*
bo	*he, she, it will be*	bodo (bojo)	*they will be*

You combine these forms with a verb's past participle (which we learnt about in the last unit) in order to form the future tense. For example, look at these expressions from dialogues in this unit:

Naročila bom ...	I will order ...
Ne bom imela ...	I will not have ...
Boš kaj pila?	Will you drink something?

Remember!

How to

- say that you like something:

  use the verb **imeti** and the adjective **rad**, e.g.

Kaj imaš rada?	What do you like?
Rada imam klasično glasbo.	I like classical music.

- say that you like doing something:

  use the adjective **rad** and the verb in the correct personal ending, e.g.

Kaj rad delaš?	What do you like doing?
Rad poslušam klasično glasbo.	I like listening to classical music.

- ask how someone is feeling and say how you feel:

Kako se počutite?	How do you feel?
Dobro/slabo se počutim.	I feel well/ill (lit. badly).

- use the future tense

  The verb **biti**, 'to be', forms the future tense as follows:

singular	plural
1 bom	bomo
2 boš	boste
3 bo	bodo (bojo)

For all other verbs, use the future tense of **biti** and a past participle.

Exercises

1   You want to say that you like the food and drinks shown below. Put the nouns into the correct case.

   a   Rad imam (*white coffee*)
   b   Raje imam (*tea with milk*)
   c   Najraje imam (*white wine*)

2   You are asked what you like doing in your spare time. Say that you:

   a   like listening to classical music
   b   like travelling
   c   like watching TV

3   Your friend looks a bit off colour. How would you ask him how he is feeling?

4   You are on a business trip abroad and a full diary has been arranged for you. You want to add a few private notes to it. Write them down in Slovene.

   a   On Monday I must telephone my wife.
   b   On Wednesday I must write a short letter to my secretary.
   c   On Friday I must buy a present for my wife.

5   What kind of music do you like? Say which of the following you like listening to, which you prefer, and which you like most:

   pop glasba   plesna glasba (*dance music*)
   klasična glasba   folklorna glasba
   jazz   rock and roll

6   You have just been offered something to eat. How would you say 'No, thank you, I'm not hungry'?

7   You have ordered a sandwich in a bar, and the waiter asks if you'd like something to drink. Tell him that you will not have anything just now, but that you will order a coffee later.

8   You look a bit **zaskrbljen** and a friend says to you **Ne skrbi!** What does she mean?

9   You are making plans for the future. Write down what you will do:

   a   this evening   c   next month
   b   tomorrow   d   next year

And something else ...

Irena has accompanied Sara to the airport. Once Irena has checked in, they have a cup of coffee before Irena flies off.

Irena Mi boš pisala?

Sara Seveda ti bom pisala. Danes zvečer ti bom telefonirala in ti povedala, kako sem potovala.

Irena Lepo. Ali boš pogrešala Slovenijo?

Sara Mislim, da. Zelo mi je bilo všeč. Hvala ti za vse.

Irena Ni za kaj! Škoda, da ne ostaneš še en mesec. In škoda, da je bilo skoraj ves čas slabo vreme.

Sara Ja, ampak kljub temu je bilo lepo. Sedaj si ti na vrsti, da me prideš obiskat.

Irena Mogoče naslednje leto. Prihraniti bom morala nekaj denarja.

pogrešati	*to miss*
Hvala ti za vse.	*Thank you for everything.*
škoda	*a pity*
ostati	*to stay*
kjub temu	*in spite of that*
Sedaj si ti na vrsti.	*Now it's your turn.*
prihraniti	*to save*
nekaj denarja	*some money*

08
želite, prosim?
how may I help you?

In this unit you will learn
- how to do your shopping
- how to use expressions relating to needs and desire
- how to use the genitive case
- how to express 'would'

► Dialogues

V pekarni *(At the bakery)*

A customer is at the bakery counter, buying bread.

Prodajalka	Kdo je na vrsti?
Stranka	Mislim, da sem jaz.
Prodajalka	Kako vam lahko postrežem?
Stranka	Želel bi hleb rženega, štruco belega in štiri žemlje prosim.
Prodajalka	Izvolite. Želite še kaj drugega?
Stranka	Ali imate francoski kruh?
Prodajalka	Na žalost ne več.
Stranka	Potem bi bilo to vse, hvala.

pekarna: v pekarni	*bakery: at the bakery*
prodajalka	*shop assistant*
stranka	*customer (**stranka** can also mean client)*
Kdo je na vrsti?	*Whose turn is it?*
Kako vam lahko postrežem?	*How may I help you?*
hleb	*a loaf (round)*
rženega	*ryebread*
štruca	*a loaf (oval)*
belega	*white bread*
žemlje	*bread rolls*
Želite še kaj drugega?	*Would you like anything else?*
francoski kruh	*French bread*
Na žalost ne več.	*I'm afraid there's none left*
Potem bi bilo to vse.	*Then that would be all.*

▶V mesnici (At the butcher's)

A customer is at the meat counter and wants some pork chops and mince for a barbecue.

Mesar	Prosim?
Stranka	Deset svinjskih kotletov, ne mastnih, prosim, in en kilogram govejega in en kilogram svinjskega mletega, prosim.
Mesar	Želite še kaj?
Stranka	To bi bilo vse, hvala.

svinjski kotlet	*pork chop*
masten	*fatty*
en kilogram	*one kilo*
govejega	*beef*
svinjskega	*pork*
mleto meso: mletega	*mince: of mince*
Želite še kaj?	*Would you like anything else?*
To bi bilo vse.	*That will be all.*

Did you understand?

a What does the customer buy at the bakery?
b What does the customer buy at the butcher's?

Did you know?

1 Po nakupih (Shopping)

Small shops where you ask for things at a counter still exist, but have become rather rare in recent years. As elsewhere, large self-service supermarkets (**samopostrežna trgovina**), hypermarkets (**hypermarket**) and department stores (**veleblagovnica**) where you can buy everything, not only food, are now the commonest places to go shopping. For this reason you can shop perfectly well without knowing a word of Slovene.

2 Mere (Measures)

The following measures are used when buying food. Fruit and vegetables are priced per kilo and liquids per litre.

mera	measure
kilogram	(kg)
pol kilograma	(1/2 kg)
dekagram	(dkg)
gram	(g)
liter	(l)
deciliter	(dl)

▶ 3 Sadje in zelenjava *(Fruit and vegetables)*

Here are some words for fruit and vegetables:

Sadje *(fruit)*		**Zelenjava** *(vegetables)*	
jabolka	apples	zelje	cabbage
hruške	pears	korenje	carrots
marelice	apricots	cvetača	cauliflower
breskve	peaches	gobe	mushrooms
slive	plums	fižol	beans
grozdje	grapes	grah	peas

Almost every town and village has a market (**tržnica**) where you can buy fresh fruit and vegetables. They are mostly seasonal.

4 Specialist shops

Here are the words for some specialist shops. You will find many of these within larger department stores:

čistilnica	*dry cleaners*
fotograf	*photographic shop*
frizer	*hairdresser*
knjigarna	*bookshop*
lekarna	*pharmacy*
mesnica	*butcher's*
pekarna	*bakery*
slaščičarna	*cake shop*
spominki	*gift-shop*
trafika	*tobacconist*
tržnica	*market*

5 Ribe *(Fish)*

You can buy fish at markets and at covered markets, where you have to look for **ribarnica** *(fishmonger's)*. Trout is probably the most commonly eaten fish in Slovenia, and is not expensive. At every fish counter as well as on every restaurant menu you will probably see the *words* **sveže postrvi** *(fresh trout)*. Some other names for fish are:

školjke	*shellfish*
raki	*lobster*
lignje	*squid*
kalamari	*octopus*

6 Meso *(Meats)*

Traditional Slovene dishes are quite meaty, although in recent years a number of vegetarian restaurants have opened and there is an increasing demand for **brezmesne jedi** *(meatless dishes)*. Pork is eaten most; the killing of a pig is a traditional event in Slovenia. Here are the words for a few other meats:

raca	*duck*
zajec	*rabbit*
piščanec	*chicken*
govedina	*beef*

7 Kruh (Bread)

There is a wide choice of different breads, which vary from region to region. The important words to know in a bakery are:

beli kruh	*white bread*
črni kruh	*brown bread*
rženi kruh	*rye bread*
žemlje	*bread rolls*

Notice that brown bread is called literally 'black bread'.

8 Mleko in mlečni izdelki (Milk and dairy products)

9 Bi ...? (Would ...?)

As you have already gathered 'bi' means *'would'*. Bi normally expresses a possibility or a hypothesis, and you will see in the next unit how easily conditional clauses are constructed in Slovene.

In addition, **bi** is used in certain phrases, a few of which you have already come across. Sentences such as, *'Would you like a coffee?'* are expressed by **Bi kavo?** which means literally, *'Would coffee?'* but it is understood who you are referring to, and that you are asking them whether they would like a coffee. The noun which follows **bi** will be in the accusative case.

In the dialogues you came across the expressions **'Bi še kaj drugega?** *(Would you like anything else?)'* and **'To bi bilo vse'** *(That would be all)*. Again, these are commonly used phrases.

When you want to say that you would like something, you use the verb **želeti** *(to want, to desire)* and say:

| Želel bi ... | *I would like ...* (if you are a man) |
| Želela bi ... | *I would like ...* (if you are a woman) |

10 The genitive case

- When you express a quantity of something, e.g. a loaf of bread, you do not translate the preposition *'of'*; the word which follows *'of'* is put into the genitive case, for example:

hleb kruha	*a loaf (of) bread*
kilogram mesa	*1kg (of) meat*
liter mleka	*1 l (of) milk*

- Other words which express quantity, like **veliko, malo, nekaj, koliko, toliko** are also followed by the noun in the genitive case, for example:

Koliko kruha želite?	*How much bread would you like?*
Imam veliko dela.	*I have a lot of work.*
Ostalo mi je še nekaj denarja.	*I still have some money left.*
Rad bi še malo mleka.	*I would like a bit more milk.*

- The genitive case is also used for the direct object of all negative verbs. This means that *whenever you negate, the noun will be in the genitive case*. Compare the following sentences:

Rad pijem kavo.	*I like drinking coffee.*
Ne pijem kave.	*I do not drink coffee.*
Jutri imam čas.	*I have time tomorrow.*
Jutri **ni**mam časa.	*I do not have time tomorrow.*
Poznaš Sonjo?	*Do you know Sonja?*
Ne poznam Sonje.	*I do not know Sonja.*

Also, whenever **ni** is placed next to a noun, the noun will be in the genitive case, as in:

Kruha **ni** na mizi.	*Bread is not on the table.*
Očeta še **ni** doma.	*Father is not home yet.*

- When a noun comes after the following prepositions it will be in the genitive case:

od (*from*)
do (*until*)
iz (*from*)
zaradi (*because of*)
blizu (*near*)
namesto (*instead of*)
sredi (*in the middle of*)

Here are a few examples:

od Ljubljane **do** Bleda	*from Ljubljana to Bled*
iz Londona	*from London*
zaradi slabega vremena	*because of bad weather*
blizu tebe	*near you*
namesto mene	*instead of me*
sredi mesta	*in the middle of town*

The basic rules for the genitive case are:

- Feminine nouns ending in –a change their ending to –e.
- Masculine and neuter nouns change their ending to –a.

11 Double negative

Negative words like **nič** (*nothing*), **nihče** (*nobody*), **nikoli** (*never*), take a negative verb. This is called *double negative*, and whilst it is wrong to use such a construction in English, you *must* use it in Slovene. Here are a few examples:

Nič ne vem o tem.	*I know nothing about this.* (lit. *I don't know nothing about this.*)
Nihče ni prišel.	*Nobody came.* (lit. *Nobody didn't come.*)
Nikoli ne veš.	*You never know.* (lit. *You don't never know.*)

Remember!

How to

- say that you would like something:

Želel bi ...	I'd like ...
Želela bi še ...	I'd also like ...
Imate ...?	Do you have ...?

- use measures:

kilogram (kg)
gram (g)
liter (l)
deciliter (dl)

- offer someone a drink:

Bi kavo?	Would you like a coffee?
Bi raje čaj?	Would you prefer some tea?
Bi kozarec vina?	Would you like a glass of wine?

Exercises

1 Here are some common foods. Match the Slovene with the English equivalent.

a	beli kruh	1	brown bread
b	meso	2	chicken
c	žemlje	3	fish
d	piščanec	4	fruit
e	črni kruh	5	bread rolls
f	ribe	6	milk
g	mleko	7	meat
h	sadje	8	white bread

2 You have the items below on your shopping list. How will you ask for the given quantity of these items?

a 1 kg of apples
b ½ l of red wine
c 1 l of milk
d ½ kg of mince

3 a A shop assistant asks you if you would like anything else. How does she say that?
b Tell her that that will be all, thank you.

4   You want to go to some specialist shops to make some purchases. Say the name of the shop where you will go if:

   a   you need a dictionary
   b   you want some fresh pork chops
   c   you want some fresh rolls for breakfast
   d   you need your shirt cleaned

5   You have a rather fussy guest at home. Ask her if she would like:

   a   a coffee
   b   whether she would prefer tea
   c   a juice
   d   a glass of wine

▶ 6   You are waiting for your turn at the market stall. A *greengrocer*, **branjevka**, has just finished serving a customer. What will you hear her say to ask who is next?

▶ 7   You are at the bread counter in the supermarket. It is your turn. The shop assistant says, '**Želite, prosim?**' You would like a round loaf of brown bread and an oval loaf of white bread. Ask for them.

8   Which one of the following words is the odd one out? **korenje, fižol, raca, cvetača, grah.**

9   Fill in the missing words as indicated:

   a   kozarec (*of red wine*)
   b   konec (*of the month*)
   c   začetek (*of the week*)
   d   skodelica (*of coffee*)

And something else ...

Every good cook knows how important *herbs*, **začimbe**, are. Here is a short passage on **peteršilj**, *parsley*.

Peteršilj je začimba in uporabljamo jo kot dodatek jedem, zlasti juham, prikuham in različnim omakam. Zelo pa izboljša okus tudi pečenemu mlademu krompirju, različnim solatam, rižu in tudi drugim jedem. S peteršiljem okrasimo narezke, različne mesne jedi in prikuhe. Sveži listi peteršilja so pomemben vir vitamina C.

Ker peteršilja ni zahtevno gojiti, bi bilo prav, da bi ga našli v vsakem vrtu, ker je odlična začimba, pomaga pa nam tudi ohranjati zdravje.

dodatek	*accessory*
jedem (dative)	*(to) dishes*
zlasti	*particularly*
juha	*soup*
mlad krompir	*new potatoes*
različne solate	*various salads*
riž	*rice*
okrasiti	*to decorate*
narezek	*a plate of sliced meats and cheeses*
mesne jedi	*meat dishes*
prikuhe	*side orders*
sveži listi peteršilja	*fresh parsley leaves*
pomemben vir vitamina C	*important source of vitamin C*
zahtevno	*demanding*
gojiti	*to grow, to cultivate*
ohranjati zdravje	*keep our health*

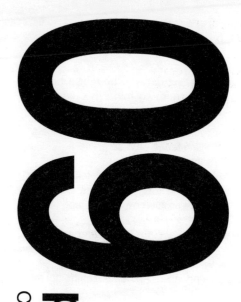

09

pridite na obisk!
come and see us!

In this unit you will learn
- how to express an hypothesis
- how to accept or refuse an invitation
- how to describe a room, your house or flat
- how to use perfective and imperfective verbs
- how to use possessive adjectives

▶ Dialogues

Povabilo *(Invitation)*

Tatjana and her family have sold their flat and bought a house just out of town. She telephones Brigita to invite her and her family to see their new house.

Tatjana	Pozdravljena, Brigita. Kličem te, ker sem vas želela povabiti na večerjo. Prejšnji teden smo se preselili.
Brigita	Čestitke! Ali je v hiši že vse gotovo?
Tatjana	Kje pa! Videla boš, kako je. In zaenkrat bo tudi tako ostalo. Manjka še ogromno stvari in zmanjkuje nam denarja. Vem, da nas čaka še veliko problemov, ampak lepo je biti v svoji hiši.
Brigita	Razumem, ampak to ni pomembno. Prepričana sem, da se bo vse uredilo.
Tatjana	Želite priti naokrog v petek okoli pol osmih?
Brigita	Ja, z veseljem! Hvala za povabilo! Preden pozabim, daj mi novi naslov.

povabilo	*invitation*
povabiti	*to invite*
preseliti se: smo se preselili	*to move: we have moved*
čestitke	*congratulations*
Ali je v hiši že vse gotovo?	*Is everything ready yet in the house?*
Kje pa!	*Not at all!*
zaenkrat	*for the time being*
bo tudi tako ostalo	*it will stay so*
manjkati	*to be missing*
ogromno	*very many*
stvari	*things*
Zmanjkuje nam denarja.	*We are getting short of money.*
v svoji hiši	*in one's own house*
to ni pomembno	*this is not important*
prepričana sem	*I'm sure*
Vse se bo uredilo.	*Everything will be fine.*
priti naokrog	*come around*
preden pozabim	*before I forget*
Daj mi novi naslov.	*Give me your new address.*

As Brigita and her family arrive, Tatjana shows them around the house and tells them one or two things about it.

Tatjana	To je dnevna soba. Marjan je sam položil tapete in tudi parket.
Brigita	Lepa in velika soba je.
Tatjana	Tukaj bo jedilnica ampak zaenkrat je še prazna.
Brigita	Ta soba je še večja. Zelo lep razgled na vrt imate.
Tatjana	Ja, če bi še enkrat začeli, bi bila to dnevna soba.
Brigita	Oh, to je vedno tako. Če bi imeli mi več denarja, bi tudi veliko spremenili.
Tatjana	In tukaj je kuhinja, manjkajo še zavese in nov štedilnik. Naročili smo ga že pred šestimi tedni in ga še niso pripeljali.
Brigita	Ja, vem, kakšni problemi so z vsemi temi stvarmi. Ko smo mi naročili pralni stroj, je prišlo do neke pomote in namesto pralnega stroja so nam pripeljali pomivalni stroj. Potrpežljiv moraš biti, ko se preseliš. In koliko sob je zgoraj?
Tatjana	Tri spalnice in kopalnica.

dnevna soba	*living-room*
polagati tapete	*to lay wallpaper*
parket	*parquet floor*
jedilnica	*dining-room*
prazna	*empty*
večja	*bigger*
razgled	*view*
vrt	*garden*
če bi še enkrat začeli …	*if we were starting again …*
če bi imeli več denarja …	*if we had more money …*
spremeniti	*to change*
kuhinja	*kitchen*
manjkati	*to miss*
zavese	*curtains*
štedilnik	*cooker*
naročiti	*to order*
pred šestimi tedni	*six weeks ago*
Ga še niso pripeljali.	*They still haven't delivered it.*
pralni stroj	*washing machine*
pomota	*mistake*
namesto	*instead of*
pomivalni stroj	*dishwasher*
potrpežljiv	*patient*
spalnica	*bedroom*
kopalnica	*bathroom*

Did you understand?

a What is the layout of Tatjana's new house?
b What happened to Brigita when she ordered her washing machine?

Did you know?

1 Housing in Slovenia

After the Second World War, many blocks of flats (**blok** *sg.* **bloki** *pl.*) were built in larger towns, often on the outskirts, and new districts, **naselja**, were created. Near to the centre of towns there are terraced houses, **vrstne hiše**, although they differ in style from English ones.

vrata

stoli

jedilnǐsko pohǐstvo

-*velika izbira*
-*krediti*
-*privlačne cene*

vrata	doors
stoli	chairs
jedilniško pohištvo	dining-room furniture
velika izbira	large choice
krediti	loans
privlačne cene	inviting prices

In villages you will find streets of private family houses. Most of them have been built since the war and have a bit of land around them. It is common to build one's own house, a process which involves buying a patch of land, obtaining permission, and then building. These private houses continue to be built.

Slovenes give the size of their flats or houses in square metres. When buying a house or flat, one would usually know the going rate per square metre in a particular area.

2 Zgoraj / spodaj (Up / down)

Zgoraj means *up* and **spodaj** means *down*. These words are used to express *upstairs* and *downstairs*, for example:

| Kje je kuhinja? | *Where is the kitchen?* |
| Zgoraj. | *Upstairs.* |

| Kje je kopalnica? | *Where is the bathroom?* |
| Spodaj. | *Downstairs.* |

3 Possessive adjectives and the use of *svoj*

Possessive adjectives are not used as much in Slovene as in English; they are unnecessary when we know who owns what we are referring to, for example:

| Imaš ključ? | *Do you have (your) key?* |
| Ja, v žepu ga imam. | *Yes, it is in (my) pocket.* |

Svoj means *one's own*. Look at the following examples:

He has his key in his pocket.
Tatjana showed us her house.

In both of these sentences there is a possibility of misunderstanding, since he could have someone else's key in his pocket, or Tatjana could have shown us another woman's house. Both *his* and *her* in the sentences above would be translated by **svoj**, which takes adjectival endings:

On ima **svoj** ključ v žepu.
Tatjana nam je pokazala **svojo** hišo.

4 Use of tenses

When you answer an English question which asks you how long something has been happening, such as: '*How long have you been living here?*' the question is in the past tense. In Slovene, the question is in the present tense: '**Kako dolgo že stanujete tukaj?**' Here are a few more examples:

Kako dolgo že delate tukaj?   *How long have you been working here?*
Kako dolgo ste že v Ljubljani? *How long have you been in Ljubljana?*

5 Use of *že* (already)

The small word **že** which appears in all the Slovene sentences above means *already* and is very commonly used, in both questions and answers. The answers to the questions above would be:

Že osem let.   *For eight years (already).*
Že pet tednov.   *For five weeks (already).*

6 Use of *šele* and *samo* (only)

Whilst **že** implies that something has been happening for quite a while, **šele** means *only*. **Samo** also means *only*, but **samo** and **šele** are not interchangeable in Slovene. You will learn the difference between them. Look at these examples:

Kdaj si prišel?   *When did you come?*
Šele včeraj.   Only *yesterday.*

Kako dolgo ostaneš? *For how long will you stay?*
Samo dva dni.   Only *two days.*

7 Completed and uncompleted actions

All Slovene verbs take two forms: perfective and imperfective. Compare these two columns:

Perfective	Imperfective
položiti	polagati
začeti	začenjati
zmanjkati	zmanjkovati
urediti	urejati
oditi	odhajati
prodati	prodajati
kupiti	kupovati

The perfective verb is a shortened version of the imperfective. The imperfective implies an action which is continuous. The sentences listed below will help you to understand the meaning and usage of these verbs:

Že odhajaš?	*Are you leaving already?*
Kdaj je odšel?	*When did he leave?*
Kaj prodajajo tukaj?	*What are they selling here?*
Kaj kupuješ?	*What are you buying?*
Prodali smo stanovanje in kupili hišo.	*We sold our flat and bought a house.*

8 Conditional

Here are two examples of how to express a condition in Slovene:

| Če bi vedel ... | *If I knew ...* |
| Če ne bi deževalo ... | *If it hadn't rained ...* |

In Slovene the conditional is formed with 'bi' + *past participle*. Conditional sentences usually start with **če** *if*.

The phrase **lahko bi** renders the meaning of '*could*', as in:

| Lahko bi mi pomagal. | *You could help me.* |
| Lahko bi šli v Ameriko. | *We could go to America.* |

Note the use of '**bi**' in these examples:

| Če **bi** imela več časa, **bi** ti pomagala. | *If I had more time I would help you.* |

Če ne **bi** bil ves dan v službi, bi sam položil tapete.

If I hadn't been at work all day I would put on the wallpaper myself.

Če **bi** imel več denarja, **bi** kupil večjo hišo.

If I had more money I would buy a bigger house.

Remember!

How to

- invite somebody around:

  Želel sem te / vas povabiti ... *I wanted to invite you ...*
  Rada bi te / vas povabila ... *I'd like to invite you ...*

- accept/refuse an invitation

  Z veseljem, hvala! *With pleasure, thank you.*
  Žal mi je, ampak ... *I'm sorry, but ...*

- show someone around your flat/house:

  pokazati stanovanje / hišo *to show a flat / house*
  (+ dative) *(to someone)*

- describe rooms in your dwelling:

soba	*room*
kuhinja	*kitchen*
dnevna soba	*living-room*
jedilnica	*dining-room*
spalnica	*bedroom*
kopalnica	*bathroom*

Exercises

1 Below are words for rooms in a house or flat. Match the English and Slovene words.

a reception room   1 kuhinja
b bedroom   2 kopalnica
c kitchen   3 dnevna soba
d bathroom   4 jedilnica
e dining-room   5 spalnica

2 In which room would you fit the following? **pralni stroj, pomivalni stroj, štedilnik.**

3 How would you ask someone how big his flat is?

4 Could you tell a Slovene the size of your flat or house in square metres?

5 Could you describe your flat or house to a Slovene friend? Tell him how many rooms you have, what they are and where they are.

▶ **6** You are invited to supper. How would you say thank you for the invitation?

7 You meet a friend whom you haven't seen for a while. Ask him how long he has been living here.

8 If a friend tells you: '**Preselil sem se**', what has he done?

▶ **9** You want to invite a Slovene to your house for lunch. What would you say?

10 Fill in the correct form (perfective or imperfective) of the verb given in brackets. In one of the sentences, both forms may be used.

a Ste že — novo hišo? (kupiti, kupovati)
b — okno, prosim. (zapreti, zapirati)
c Kaj delaš? — stanovanje. (pospravljati, pospraviti)
d V kateri trgovini — (kupiti, kupovati)
e Lani smo — več kot predlani. (izvoziti, izvažati)

And something else ...

Pohištvo za plitev žep (Furniture for a shallow pocket)

Vsak začetek je težak, tudi prvo stanovanje prinaša poleg veselja kup problemov. Ste porabili ves denar za nakup stanovanja ali hiše? Bi se radi vselili in opremili sobe? V tem primeru se je najbolje odločiti za prehodno pohištvo, ki mora biti predvsem poceni, dobro pa je, če ga lahko tudi kasneje uporabimo.

Vsak začetel je težak.	lit. *Every beginning is difficult.*
prvo stanovanje	*the first flat*
prinaša	*brings*
poleg veselja	*apart from joy* (lit. *next to joy*)
kup problemov	*a lot of problems*
porabiti ves denar	*to spend all the money*
za nakup stanovanja	*for the purchase of the flat*
ali hiše	*or house*
vseliti se	*to move in*
opremiti sobe	*to furnish rooms*
v tem primeru	*in this case*
Se je najbolje odločiti …	*It is best to go for …*
prehodno pohištvo	*temporary furniture*
predvsem	*above all, particularly*
dobro pa je	*but it is good*
kasneje uporabiti	*to use later*

10

dober tek!

bon appétit!

In this unit you will learn
- how to order a meal in a restaurant
- how to find the best place to eat
- how to follow a recipe in Slovene
- how to use the instrumental case

▶ Dialogues

Nadja and Tatjana are shopping in town and have stopped for lunch at a restaurant.

Natakar	Dober dan. Mizo za dva?
Nadja	Ja, prosim. Je že pozno za kosilo?
Natakar	Ne, gospa ni. Je v redu ta miza?
Nadja	Ja.
Natakar	Izvolite jedilni list.
Nadja	Hvala. Tatjana, kaj boš pila?
Tatjana	Kozarec belega vina bi.
Nadja	Jaz bom pa eno malo pivo.
Natakar	Prav.
Nadja	Ali imate samo jedi po naročilu ali tudi že gotove jedi?
Natakar	Oboje. Tukaj je ala kart meni in na zadnji strani so današnje gotove jedi.
Nadja	Hvala. Malo bova pogledali.
Natakar	Seveda. Medtem bom prinesel pijačo.

(He comes back with drinks.)

Natakar	S čim lahko postrežem?
Nadja	Ali lahko kaj priporočite?
Natakar	Jajčevci v solati so bili vsem zelo všeč.
Nadja	Verjamem, zelo dobri so. Doma jih velikokrat pripravim.
Tatjana	Jaz pa nikoli. Ja, jaz bom jajčevce v solati in za predjed hladno paradižnikovo juho.
Natakar	Prav. In vi?
Nadja	Tudi jaz bom jajčevce, za predjed bom pa ocvrte sardine.
Natakar	Prav. Želita kakšno prilogo z glavno jedjo?
Nadja	Eno porcijo mladega praženega krompirja.
Natakar	Odlično. Ne bo dolgo trajalo. Se vama mudi?
Nadja	Ne, ampak lačni sva!

mizo za dva	*a table for two*
Je že pozno za kosilo?	*Is it too late for lunch?*
v redu	*all right, OK*
ta miza	*this table*
prav	*OK*
jedi po naročilu	*dishes to order (à la carte)*
gotove jedi	*prepared dishes*
oboje	*both*
na zadnji strani	*on the last page*
današnji, -a, -e	*today's*
Malo bova pogledali.	*We (two) will have a look.*

medtem	*in the meantime*
bom prinesel	*I'll bring*
pijača	*drinks*
S čim lahko postrežem?	*What would you like?*
	(lit. 'With what can I serve (you)?')
Ali lahko kaj priporočite?	*Can you recommend anything?*
jajčevci v solati	*aubergines in salad*
So bili vsem zelo všeč.	*Everyone liked them very much*
	(lit. 'They were to everyone
	very pleasing.')
verjeti (verjamem)	*to believe*
pripraviti (pripravim)	*to prepare*
predjed	*starter*
hladna paradižnikova juha	*cold tomato soup*
ocvrte sardine	*fried sardines*
priloga	*side dish*
porcija	*portion*
mlad pražen krompir	*fried new potatoes*
odlično	*excellent*
Ne bo dolgo trajalo.	*It won't be long.*
Se vama mudi?	*Are you (two) in a hurry?*
Lačni sva.	*We (two) are hungry.*

Note. *As the waiter was addressing two women there were quite a few dual forms used in this dialogue. You will hear these forms used, and you will tune into them with time.*

Jajčevci v solati *(Aubergine salad)*

Nadja and Tatjana enjoyed their main course very much. Nadja told Tatjana how to prepare aubergines like that, as she often cooks them at home for her family.

Za 4 osebe potrebuješ:

50 dkg manjših jajčevcev, sol, 6 strokov česna, 1,5 dl olja, 1 šopek zelenega peteršilja, nekaj vejic majarona, 3/4 dl rdečega vinskega kisa, 1,5 dl čiste mesne juhe iz koncentrata (naredimo jo iz polovice kocke), sveže zmlet črn poper, 25 dkg majhnih paradižnikov.

Jajčevce opereš, obrišeš in odrežeš peclje. Nato jih narežeš na centimeter debele rezine, po obeh straneh posoliš in razporediš na papirnate brisače. Z njimi jih tudi pokriješ. Medtem olupiš česen in stroke narežeš na tanke rezine. V večjo ponev nalijеš 4 žlice olja, ga segreješ in dodaš česen, ki ga pražiš, dokler ne postekleni. Opražen česen pobereš iz ponve in daš na krožnik. Jajčevce obrišeš s papirnatimi brisačami. V ponev priliješ del preostalega olja in ga močno segreješ. Dodaš del jajčevcev in jih pečeš najprej na eni, potem pa še na drugi strani, da dobijo svetlo rjavo barvo. Preden jih obrneš, dodaš tudi peteršiljeve in majaronove listke. Pečene jajčevce pobereš iz ponve in daš v veliko skledo. Postopek pečenja jajčevcev ponavljaš, dokler ne spečeš vseh jajčevče. Pri pečenju porabiš ves peteršilj, majarona pa le polovico. Pečene jajčevče v skledi potreseš s pripravljenim česnom. Na olje, ki je ostalo v ponvi, naliješ kis in juho, zavreš, popopraš in po želji tudi osladiš. Gotov preliv zliješ na jajčevce, skledo pokriješ in daš za 2 uri na hladno, da jajčevci vpijejo preliv. Malo preden solato ponudiš, opereš paradižnike, jih narežeš na četrtine ali osmine (odvisno od velikosti), posoliš in skupaj s preostalo polovico majaronovih listkov rahlo primešaš jajčevcem.

Solata je nasitna, ponudiš jo lahko samo s kruhom. Dobra je tudi kot priloga k mesu z žara in kot predjed.

Did you understand?

What were Nadja's and Tatjana's orders for food and drink in the restaurant?

Did you know?

1 Hungry/thirsty

These are words that spring to mind when talking about food, so let's revise them.

biti **lačen, –čna, –čni** *to be hungry*, biti **žejen, –jna, –jni** *to be thirsty*

Lačen in žejen je.	*He is hungry and thirsty.*
Si lačna ali žejna?	*Are you hungry or thirsty?* (when asking a woman)
Vsi smo lačni in žejni.	*We are all hungry and thirsty.*

2 Meals

Slovenes are not big breakfast eaters: a cup of coffee and perhaps something small is all that is commonly eaten in the morning. They do have a snack of some sort, **malica**, at about 11 a.m. Traditionally lunch was the meal of the day, but with changing working hours (people now start and finish work later) families have the main meal of the day after work, at about four, five or six o'clock. In the evenings only a snack will be eaten. Of course, the pattern of eating differs from one family to another, depending on their lifestyle.

The names of meals are:

zajtrk	*breakfast*
kosilo	*lunch*
večerja	*supper*

The word for *a snack* is **malica**.

▶ 3 Courses and types of food

Because of the changing climate (usually cold winters and hot summers) different foods are eaten in different seasons. In the winter it is almost a rule to have soup for a starter, followed by 'winter dishes', whilst lighter dishes are served in spring and summer.

The words for courses of a meal are:

predjed	*starter*
hladne predjedi	*cold starters*
tople predjedi	*hot starters*
glavna jed	*main meal/course*
sladica *or* **desert**	*dessert*

4 Places to eat

As elsewhere, you will find a number of different places to eat, from simple snack bars where you stand to eat, to more extravagant restaurants. The most common places to eat are:

- **restavracija** (*restaurant*); they vary enormously
- **samopostrežna restavracija** (*self-service restaurant*); they serve both snacks and hot meals
- **bife** (*snack bar*); found at stations and in towns. One usually stands and has a drink and a snack
- **gostilna** (*inn*); they vary, from down- to up-market ones. It is worth asking for a recommendation of a good **gostilna**. Some of them serve homemade traditional food

There are also many international-style places to eat, and you will need no help in finding those.

5 Jedilni pribor (Cutlery)

The words for cutlery are:

žlica	spoon
vilice (pl.)	fork
nož	knife
žlička	teaspoon

Their endings change as follows:

z žlic**o**	with a spoon
z vilic**ami**	with a fork
z nož**em**	with a knife
z žlič**ko**	with a teaspoon

6 If being a guest gets difficult

The word for '*guest*' is **gost** (sg.)/**gostje** (pl.) It is not difficult to be a guest in a restaurant or places where you pay for being a guest; it can, however, be less easy in people's houses. Here are some phrases you can use to show respect and approval.

Lepo hišo/stanovanje imate!

Lep vrt imate!

When at the table, you may come across the word **domač**, **–a**, **–e**. It means homemade. Many Slovenes will preserve various fruits and vegetables in the seasons when they grow and keep them through the year.

Je to domač, –a, –e ...?	
So to domači ...?	*Is this/are these homemade?*
Zelo dobro(–a) je. Zelo dobri so.	*It is/they are very good.*

When you are offered more food or drink but don't want any more, you can say:

Ne hvala, ampak bilo je zelo dobro.	*No, thank you, but it was very good.*
Ne hvala, ne morem več.	*No, thank you, I can't eat any more.*

Hvala, sit/sita sem.   *Thank you, I'm full.*
Res ne morem več.   *I really can't eat any more.*

7 Ali ... ali *(Either ... or)* Ne ... ne ... *(Neither ... nor ...)*

You know that **ali** can be a question indicator and can also mean '*or*'. If you want to say *either ... or ...*, you use **ali ... ali**, for example:

ali solato ali zelenjavo   *either salad or vegetables*
ali vsi ali nihče   *either everybody or no-one*

Ne means '*no, not*'. To express *neither ... nor* you use **ne ... ne**, for example:

Nisem ne lačen ne žejen.   *I am neither hungry*
                              nor thirsty.
Ne pijejo ne piva ne vina.   *They drink neither beer*
                              nor wine.

8 The instrumental case

The instrumental case is mainly used as the object of certain prepositions; nouns and adjectives governed by these prepositions take the endings that correspond to this case.

The instrumental is most often applied when you say *with whom* or *with what* something was done.

Feminine nouns usually take an 'o' ending, masculine and neuter nouns an '**om**' or '**em**' ending. For a more comprehensive table of these endings you can refer to Appendix 1.

When you want to say *with whom* something is, has been, or will be done, you use the appropriate personal pronoun in the instrumental case, as follows:

z menoj *or* z mano	*with me*
s teboj *or* s tabo	*with you*
z njim	*with him*
z njo	*with her*
z nami	*with us*
z vami	*with you*
z njimi	*with them*

S and z both mean *'with'*. The instrumental case endings also apply with the following prepositions:

- **pred** (*before, in front of*)
  pred kosil**om**   *before lunch*
  pred hotel**om**   *in front of the hotel*

- **za** (*behind*):
  za hiš**o**   *behind the house*

- **med** (*between, among, during*):
  med **nami**   *between us, among us*
  med predstav**o**   *during the performance*

- **pod** (*under*):
  pod miz**o**   *under the table*

- **nad** (*over, above*):
  nad **to** sob**o**   *above this room*

If you are still confused about the cases and endings, do not worry! To apply every ending correctly usually takes a long time. You need to be tuned into the language, but if you can learn at least a few rules it does help.

▶ Remember!

The following phrases will be helpful if you are searching for or about to go to a restaurant:

Mi lahko priporočite kakšno dobro restavracijo?	*Can you recommend a good restaurant?*
Lahko dobim jedilni list, prosim?	*Can I have the menu, please?*
Steklenico slovenskega vina prosim.	*A bottle of Slovene wine, please.*
Imate …?	*Do you have …?*
Kaj priporočate?	*What do you recommend?*
Kaj je hišna špecialiteta?	*What is the speciality of the house?*
Kje so vegetarijanske jedi?	*Where are the vegetarian dishes?*
Kakšne solate imate?	*What salads do you have?*
Lahko dobim račun, prosim?	*Can I have the bill please?*

Exercises

▶ 1 You go to a restaurant with a friend. How would you ask for a table for two?

2 The waitress shows you to a table and says: 'Izvolite jedilni list.' What did she mean?

3 Which is the odd word out? žlica, vilice, pijača, nož.

4 You came to a bar with a group of friends and it is your turn to buy a round of drinks. Ask for the following at the bar:

   a a glass of red wine
   b a glass of white wine
   c a large beer
   d a small beer
   e a cup of white coffee with sugar
   f a fruit juice

5 Here are some dishes. Say which ones you like and which ones you don't.

   a pečen piščanec
   b mlad krompir
   c jajčevci v solati
   d zelenjavna juha
   e ribe

▶ 6 You are looking at a menu and cannot decide what to order. How would you ask a waiter whether he could recommend something?

7 Match the Slovene with the English equivalent:

   a zajtrk   1 main dish
   b kosilo   2 side dish
   c večerja   3 breakfast
   d malica   4 supper
   e predjed   5 snack
   f glavna jed   6 lunch
   g priloga   7 starter

8 You have been asked if you want seconds. Say: 'No, thank you, but it was very good.'

And something else …

If you like aubergines, and decide to make the aubergine salad for which you were given a recipe, you might want to know more about them. Read the passage below, which tells you about their origin and what you can do with them.

Jajčevci so v sorodu s paradižnikom in krompirjem, k nam pa niso prišli iz Amerike ampak iz Azije. V Indiji in na Kitajskem jih poznajo že tisočletja.

Jajčevci, kakršne dobimo pri nas, so največkrat veliki in precej zaobljeni; manjša in bolj podolgovata vrsta je manj znana. Obe imata bleščečo lupino vijoličaste barve. Toda 'prajajčevec' je bil majhen in svetle barve, po obliki in barvi je bil podoben kokošjemu jajcu in od tod ime jajčevci.

Jajčevce včasih lupimo, drugič ne. Lahko jih pečemo, pražimo, cvremo, dušimo, nadevamo – le surovih ne smemo jesti. Njihov okus je rahlo grenek. Če nas to moti, jih narežemo, posolimo in pustimo kake pol ure. Potem odcedimo tekočino in s tem tudi velik del grenkega okusa.

Najbolj slavna jed z jajčevci je verjetno grška musaka.

biti v sorodu z / s	*to be related to*
tisočletja	*thousands of years*
kakršne dobimo pri nas	*as we can buy them*
največkrat	*most of the time*
precej zaobljeni	*quite round*
bolj podolgovata vrsta	*a longer kind*
manj znana	*less known*
obe	*both*
bleščeča lupina	*shining skin*
vijoličast, –a, –o	*purple*

'prajajčevec'	'ancient aubergine'
po obliki in barvi	in shape and colour
biti podoben	to be similar to, look like
kokošje jajce	chicken's egg
od tod ime	hence the name
včasih lupimo, drugič ne	sometimes we peel, and other times not
peči	to bake
pražiti	to fry, roast
cvreti	to fry
dušiti	to stew
nadevati	to stuff
surov, –a, –o	raw
ne smemo jesti	must not eat
okus	taste
rahlo grenek	slightly bitter
motiti	to disturb
narezati	to slice
posoliti	to sprinkle with salt
pustiti kake pol ure	to leave for about half an hour
odcediti	to filter off
tekočina	liquid
s tem tudi	with that also
velik del grenkega okusa	most of the bitterness
najbolj slavna jed	the most famous dish
verjetno	probably
grška musaka	Greek moussaka

11
kakšno bo jutri vreme?
what will the weather be like tomorrow?

In this unit you will learn
- how to use more words and phrases describing the weather
- how to read and understand weather forecasts
- how to use impersonal expressions
- how to use the points of the compass
- how to use the locative case

▶ Dialogues

Gremo na izlet! *(Let's go for a trip!)*

A group of friends meet in a bar to discuss how to go away for a few days to Kranjska Gora at Easter. See what Matjaž and Igor come up with.

Matjaž Pomlad je in gotovo bo toplo!

Igor Kar se tiče vremena, človek nikoli ne ve! Ampak vsi bomo imeli nahrbtnike in planinsko opremo.

Matjaž Seveda. S kolesom se bomo odpeljali do planinskega doma Tram in tam prenočili. Naslednji dan se bomo naprej odpravili peš. Predlagam, da na dan napravimo približno 25 kilometrov.

Igor Strinjam se. Jaz imam natančen opis poti s kartami in tudi podrobnimi infor-macijami o tem, kje lahko med potjo jemo, prenočimo in drugo.

Matjaž Ali imaš tudi kakšen leksikon, v katerem so opisane pomembne znamenitosti, ki so ob poti?

Igor Imam. Mitja mi ga je posodil. Vse bom izpisal in prinesel zraven. Pozanimati se moramo še, kakšna je vremenska napoved.

Gotovo bo toplo.	*It will surely be warm.*
kar se tiče vremena	*as far as weather is concerned*
Človek nikoli ne ve.	*One never knows.*
nahrbtnik	*rucksack*
planinska oprema	*hiking kit*
kolo: s kolesom	*bike: by bike*
odpeljati se	*to ride away*
planinski dom	*guesthouse in the mountains*
prenočiti	*to stay the night*
odpraviti se	*to set off*
napraviti približno	*to do approximately*
x kilometrov	*x kilometres*

strinjati se	*to agree*
natančen opis poti	*exact description of the way*
karta: s kartami	*map: with maps*
podrobne informacije	*detailed information*
med potjo	*on the way*
opisati pomembne znamenitosti	*describe important sites*
ob poti	*on the way*
izpisati si	*to write out*
prinesti zraven	*to bring with oneself*
pozanimati se	*to inform oneself*

Vremenska napoved *(Weather forecast)*

Igor looked in a newspaper to see what the weather forecast was.

jasno

NAPOVED ZA SLOVENI-JO – Precej jasno bo, občasno ponekod zmerno oblačno. Najvišje dnevne temperature bodo od 20 do 25, na Primorskem okoli 28 stopinj C.

OBETI – V petek in soboto bo večinoma jasno z občasno zmerno oblačnostjo.

VREMENSKA SLIKA – Nad zahodno Evropo in Skandinavijo je območje visokega zračnega pritiska. Nad naše kraje doteka od severa suh in razmeroma hladen zrak.

TEMPERATURE MORJA – Koper 21, Poreč 23, Rovinj 22, Zadar 22, Split 22, Hvar 22.

VREME PO SLOVENIJI – Ljubljana – zmerno oblačno 21, Celje – zmerno oblačno 21, Murska Sobota – zmerno oblačno 22, Novo mesto – delno oblačno 20, Kočevje – pretežno oblačno 19, Postojna – delno oblačno 21, Portorož – pretežno oblačno 27, Nova Gorica – delno oblačno 24, Vogel – pretežno oblačno 11, Kredarica – pretežno oblačno 8 stopinj C.

napoved	*forecast*
Hidrometeorološki zavod Slovenije	*equiv. of Meteorological Office*
jasno	*clear*
občasno	*at times*
ponekod	*in some places*
zmerno oblačno	*partly overcast*
najvišje dnevne temperature	*maximum day temperature*
obeti	*forecast*
večinoma	*mostly*
z občasno zmerno oblačnostjo	*with patchy clouds*
vremenska slika	*the weather forecast*
območje visokega zračnega pritiska	*the area of high pressure*
doteka nad naše kraje	*is moving towards us*
od severa	*from the north*
suh (–a, –o)	*dry*
razmeroma	*relatively*
hladen (–dna, –o)	*cold, cool*
zrak	*air*
morje	*sea*

Did you understand?

Can you explain in English what the plan for the trip to the mountains is?

Did you know?

1 The Slovene climate

The Slovene climate is Alpine, Mediterranean and Continental. Even though Slovenia is a very small country, the temperature there can vary quite a lot, since some areas are by the sea (Adriatic) and others quite high in the mountains. Summers should be very hot, and winters very cold; however, in recent years the weather has not quite followed this pattern. Due to different weather conditions during the year, outdoor activities and sports depend on the season. You can ski in winter in places where you can go for long walks or hikes in spring or summer.

2 Cycling

Cycling is popular, and you will be able to hire a bicycle in most hotels. The following words and expressions will be useful.

kolo	*bike*
gorsko kolo	*mountain bike*
kolesariti	*to cycle*
kolesarska steza	*cycle track*
najeti	*to hire*

3 Walking

Half of Slovenia is covered in forest and there are large rural areas. Most Slovene farms offer facilities for staying overnight.

You already know the verb **iti** *to go*

- If you *regularly* go somewhere, you use the verb **hoditi**:

  Ob sredah hodim na plavanje.
  I go swimming on Wednesdays.

Gozdarsko središče

- You can use **hoditi** when you *go walking*:

  Zelo rad hodim.
  I very much like walking.

Planinski dom

  Ste dolgo hodili?
  Did you walk for a long time?

Turistična kmetija

- The noun which comes from **hoditi** is **hoja**:

Hoja v hribih je zelo prijetna. *Walking in the mountains is very pleasant.*

- If you take *a short walk* you would not call it '**hoja**' but **sprehod**:

Vsako jutro grem na sprehod s psom. *I go for a walk every morning with my dog.*

4 The points of the compass

The intermediate points of the compass are:

severozahod	*northwest*
severovzhod	*northeast*
jugozahod	*southwest*
jugovzhod	*southeast*

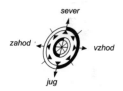

All these words will take endings according to the prepositions they are used with. Here are a few examples:

Veter piha od zahoda proti vzhodu. *The wind is blowing from west to east.*

na jugozahodni obali *on the southwest coast*

južno od ... *south of ...*

▶ 5 Understanding weather forecasts and symbols

To understand weather forecasts and to talk about the weather, you will need to know a few more words and expressions.

SONČNO

POL OBLAČNO

OBLAČNO

sončno	*sunny*
pol oblačno	*overcast*
oblačno	*cloudy*
dež	*rain*
nevihta	*storm*
megla	*fog*
sneženje	*snowing*
vetrovno	*windy*
Sončno je.	*It's sunny.*
Oblačno je.	*It's cloudy.*
Vetrovno je.	*It's windy.*
Toplo/hladno je.	*It's warm/quite cold.*
Vroče/mrzlo je.	*It's hot/cold.*

DEŽ

NEVIHTA

MEGLA

SNEŽENJE

VETROVNO

Notice that the verb, **je**, is at the end, and not at the beginning as in English.

6 Gotovo!

The word **gotovo** has two meanings, which you will be able to determine from the context. It can mean *'to be ready'*, as in:

| Vse je gotovo. | *Everything is ready.* |
| Si že gotov? | *Are you ready yet?* |

It can also mean *'certainly'*, as in:

| April je, gotovo bo nevihta. | *It's April, there will certainly be a storm.* |
| Gotovo ti bo povedal. | *He will certainly tell you.* |

7 Impersonal expressions

Impersonal expressions are those like *'you never know'*, *'one must be careful'*, etc. For such expressions Slovene uses the verb in the second person singular, or the word **človek** (*man, person*), with the verb in the third person singular, for example:

Nikoli ne **veš**.	*You never know.*
Človek nikoli ne **ve**.	*One never knows.*
Moraš biti previden.	*You must be careful.*
Človek mora biti previden.	*One must be careful.*

8 Kar se tiče ...

This is an expression meaning '*as far as – is concerned*'. It is followed by a noun in the genitive case:

Kar se tiče mene/nje/njega ...	*As far as I/she/he is concerned ...*
Kar se tiče vremena ...	*As far as the weather is concerned ...*

9 In spring, in winter ...

You know the words for the seasons. To say that something is happening in a particular season, you do not use any prepositions, but change the word as follows:

pomlad	*spring*	spomladi *or* pomladi	*in spring*	
poletje	*summer*	poleti	*in summer*	
jesen	*autumn*	jeseni, *or* v	jeseni	*in autumn*
zima	*winter*	pozimi	*in winter*	

The adjectives which come from the words for the seasons are as follows:

pomladni –a, –o *or* spomladni –a, –o	
or pomladanski –a, –o	*spring*
poletni –a, –o	*summer*
jesenski –a, –o	*autumn*
zimski –a, –o	*winter*

Here are a few examples:

Kakšen lep **jesenski dan**!	*What a lovely autumn day!*
Zimski dopust sem preživel na smučanju v Italiji.	*I spent my winter holiday skiing in Italy.*
Poletni dnevi so dolgi.	*Summer days are long.*

10 The locative case

The locative case is the last one you will hear of! Like the instrumental case, it is used as the object of certain prepositions. These are:

- **pri** (*by, at, with*):

Včeraj sem bil pri prijatel**ju**.	*I was at my friend's yesterday.*
Stanujem pri te**ti**.	*I live with my aunt.*
Vsi smo pri mi**zi**.	*We are all at the table.*

- **po** (*after, by*)

Po večer**ji** poslušam glasbo.	*I listen to music after supper.*
To je prišlo danes po poš**ti**.	*This came today by post.*

- **o** (*about*)

Kaj veš o **tem**?	*What do you know about this?*
Berem kjigo o drugi svetovni vojni.	*I am reading a book about the Second World War.*

- **ob** (*on*, in expressions of time)

ob ponedelj**kih**, tor**kih**, sreda**h**,	*on Mondays, Tuesdays, Wednesdays,*
četrt**kih**, pet**kih**, sobota**h**, nedelja**h**	*Thursdays, Fridays, Saturdays, Sundays*
ob eni**h**, dve**h**, tre**h**	*at one, two, three o'clock*
ob večeri**h**	*in the evenings*

You have often come across the prepositions '**v**' and '**na**'. They take the *locative* case when they answer the question *where?* (where something is). If they answer the question *where to?* they take the *accusative* case.

Accusative	*Locative*
Grem v kino.	Včeraj sem bila v kin**u**.
Letos gremo na dopust v Slovenijo.	Na dopus**tu** smo bili v Sloveni**ji**.
Postavi kozarce na miz**o**.	Kozarci so na mi**zi**.
Danes zvečer grem na koncert.	Kako je bilo na koncer**tu**?

- Feminine nouns take an **–i** ending in the locative.
- Masculine and neuter nouns take an **–u** ending in the locative.

For a comprehensive review of the cases look at the tables in Appendix 1.

▶ Remember!

If you decide to take advantage of Slovene 'open air' facilities, the following phrases will be useful:

Kako daleč je do ...?	*How far is it to ...?*
Kje bi lahko prenočili?	*Where could we stay overnight?*
So na poti gostilne?	*Are there inns on the way?*
Kakšno je vreme v tem letnem času?	*What is the weather like in this season?*
Ali potrebujemo ...?	*Do we need ...?*
planinsko opremo	*hiking equipment*
spalne vreče	*sleeping bags*
nepremočljive obleke	*waterproof clothing*

Exercises

1 Say that you go to work sometimes by bike, and sometimes you walk.

2 You are planning a trip to Slovenia next spring. Ask what the weather is like in Slovenia in spring.

3 If you are told: '**Oblačno je, in precej hladno**', what is the weather like?

4 Match the Slovene expressions for weather with their English equivalents:

a	Oblačno je.	**1**	It's cold.
b	Dežuje.	**2**	It's snowing.
c	Vroče je.	**3**	It's windy.
d	Hladno je.	**4**	It's cloudy.
e	Toplo je.	**5**	It's raining.
f	Sneži.	**6**	It's sunny.
g	Vetrovno je.	**7**	It's warm.
h	Sončno je.	**8**	It's hot.

5 If you were told that one place was '**severozahodno od**' another, in what direction does it lie?

6 Say that Portugal is west of Spain.

7 Which word is the odd one out, and why? **pomlad, jesenski, zima, jesen.**

8 Can you describe what the weather is like in each season?

9 A couple of friends say to you: 'Gremo na sprehod v park.' What are they suggesting?

10 You are about to go out with a few friends, but you know that Manja still has to do something. Tell your friends that Manja is not ready yet.

▶ 11 You are on holiday and want to hire a mountain bike. Complete this dialogue, which takes place at the hotel reception.

You	(*Say that you would like to hire a mountain bike.*)
Receptorka	Seveda. Za kako dolgo pa?
You	(*Say for four days. Ask how much it costs per day.*)
Receptorka	Odvisno od kolesa.
You	(*Ask if she could show you some bikes.*)
Receptorka	Samo trenutek. Poklicala bom Milana.
You	(*Ask her how far it is to town.*)
Receptorka	Približno osem kilometrov, ni daleč. Pol ure s kolesom.

And something else ...

The following article will be very useful to you if you decide to go walking in Slovenia. Don't worry if you find it difficult: this is, however, the sort of language you will come across when you start reading Slovene newspapers and other published information. This time, the vocabulary in the box will help you.

oprema	*equipment*
preskrba	*service*
prenočevanje	*overnight stay*
posebna planinska oprema	*mountaineering equipment*
upoštevati	*take into account*
hribovit, –a, –o	*mountainous*
celo	*even*
gorat, –a, –o	*mountainous*
svet	*world*
povzpeti se	*to climb*
na višine čez 1.000 metrov	*to climb above 1,000 metres*
kjer	*where*

Oprema, preskrba, prenočevanje

Na poti ne potrebujete posebne planinske opreme. Dobro pa je, če upoštevate, da boste ves čas hodili po hribovitem in celo goratem svetu; povzpeli se boste tudi na višine čez 1.000 metrov, kjer vas lahko tudi poleti vremenske spremembe kaj hitro presenetijo.

Zato popotnikom priporočamo, naj se podajo na pot v dobrih, visokih in že uhojenih čevljih in naj vzamejo s seboj dodatno perilo in obleko za primer ohladitve, ustrezno zaščito pred dežjem - vse v ne pretežkem nahrbtniku. K temu je treba dodati še sredstva za osebno higieno, majhen komplet za prvo pomoč, čutarico za vodo, jedilni pribor, beležko in svinčnik. Predvsem pa ni treba nositi s seboj preveč hrane, ker jo je mogoče sproti nabavljati v trgovinah ob poti; popotnik se bo lahko prehranjeval tudi v gostilnah, po planinskih in gozdarskih domovih ter na kmetijah.

Prenočevanje na poti je možno v planinskih domovih, v gozdarskih hišah, v hotelih, pri zasebnikih, na kmečkih domovih idr., kar je v popotni knjižici posebej omenjeno. Popotnik naj upošteva, da vodi pot po turistično manj razvitih predelih, kjer na poti ne bo deležen največje udobnosti. Zato se bo treba kdaj pa kdaj prilagoditi tudi bolj skromnim razmeram. Prepričani pa smo, da to ne bo v škodo lepim vtisom s poti. V primeru nuje pa bo seveda na poti mogoče najti zasilno prenočišče v zaselkih in po kmetijah, ki v knjižici niso posebej navedene.

vremenske spremembe	*weather changes*
kaj hitro presenetiti	*can surprise us*
popotnik: popotnikom (dative pl.)	*traveller*
podati se	*to go*
uhojeni čevlji	*worn-in shoes*
dodatno perilo	*additional clothing*
za primer ohladitve	*in case of cold weather*
ustrezna zaščita	*suitable protection*
v ne pretežkem nahrbtniku	*in a rucksack which is not too heavy*
k temu je treba dodati	*it must be added*
sredstva	*facilities*
osebna higiena	*personal hygiene*
majhen komplet za prvo pomoč	*small first aid kit*
čutarica za vodo	*water bottle*
beležka in svinčnik	*pad and pencil*
predvsem	*above all*
ni treba	*not necessary*
nositi s seboj	*to carry with you*
sproti nabavljati	*to buy when it is needed*
prehranjevati se	*to feed oneself*
planinski dom	*mountain hut*
gozdarska hiša	*forest hut*
zasebnik: pri zasebnikih	*in private houses*
kmečki dom	*farmhouse*
idr. *stands for* in drugje	*and elsewhere*
kar je	*which is*
v popotni knjižici	*in the travel guide*
posebej omenjeno	*specifically mentioned*
da vodi pot po turstično manj razvitih predelih	*that tourist-wise the route goes through less developed places*
biti deležen velike udobnosti	*to be offered great comfort*
kdaj pa kdaj	*occasionally*
prilagoditi se	*to adapt oneself, to adjust to*
bolj skromne razmere	*more basic environment*
biti prepričan	*to be sure*
biti v škodo / ne biti v škodo	*to be harmful / not to be harmful*
lepi vtisi s poti	*beautiful, impressions from the trip*
v primeru nuje	*in case of emergency*
zasilno prenočišče	*emergency lodging*
biti posebej navedeno	*to be especially mentioned*

12

ne počutim
se dobro

I don't feel well

In this unit you will learn
- how to describe how you feel
  (when you don't feel well)
- how to manage when you
  don't feel well
- how to compare things
- how to use verbs with
  prefixes

▶ Dialogues

Kako se počutiš? *(How are you feeling?)*

Simona couldn't go out with her friend Branka last night because she was not feeling well. Branka pops in to see how things are going.

Branka	Kako se počutiš?
Simona	Še vedno slabo. Glava me boli in kašljam. In zelo me zebe.
Branka	Prehladila si se. Imaš temperaturo?
Simona	Ne vem, nisem si je izmerila. Zelo sem utrujena in zaspana.
Branka	Najbolje je, de ostaneš par dni doma. Si vzela kakšen aspirin?
Simona	Ne, pijem limonin čaj.
Branka	Ali hočeš, da skočim v lekarno in ti kupim kakšne tablete?
Simona	Če imaš čas. Ampak prepričana sem, da bo čez par dni bolje.
Branka	Seveda, gripa ne traja dolgo.

prehladiti se	*to catch a cold*
imeti temperaturo	*to have a temperature*
izmeriti si temperaturo	*to take one's temperature*
najbolje je	*it is best*
ostati	*to stay*
par dni	*a few days*
vzeti aspirin	*to take aspirin*
limonin čaj	*lemon tea*
skočiti	lit. *to jump,* also *to pop*
lekarna	*pharmacy*
tablete	*tablets*
čez par dni	*in a few days*
bolje	*better*
gripa	*flu*
trajati/ne trajati	*to last/not to last*

Branka went to the chemist, bought some aspirin and picked up a leaflet with the following advice:

ZDRAVNIK SVETUJE

Vpliv prehrane na dobro počutje

V zimskih mesecih se prehranjujemo drugače kot v poletnih. Pozimi telo potrebuje nekoliko več maščobe kot v drugih letnih časih. V poletni vročini pa težka in mastna hrana ne obremenjuje le želodca, temveč dodatno ovira tudi normalno delovanje krvnega obtoka. Zato le lahka in sveža prehrana prispeva k ugodnemu počutju in zdravemu videzu. Poleti potrebujemo:

- Več sadja in sveže zelenjave in zelo malo maščob in beljakovin v obliki mesa, mesnih izdelkov, jajc, in drugih takih proizvodov
- Več tekočine v obliki navadne in mineralne vode, razredčenih sokov in zeliščnih čajev.
- Če en dan na teden ne jemo in pijemo samo sadne sokove to dodatno zagotavlja dobro delovanje prebavnih organov

Upoštevati moramo tudi naslednje:

- Pivo, vino in ostale alkoholne pijače ne sodijo med tiste pijače, ki zdravo odžejajo
- Bolniki naj se izogibajo kavi in alkoholnim pijačam, še posebej v vročih dneh. Posebej nevarne so kombinacije alkohola, kave in zdravil.

telo potrebuje	*the body needs*
maščobe	*fats*
v drugih letnih časih	*in other seasons*
težka in mastna hrana	*heavy and fat food*
ne obremenjuje le želodca	*it is not only heavy on the stomach*
temveč dodatno ovira tudi normalno	*but it also hinders your circulation*
delovanje krvnega obtoka	
lahka in sveža prehrana	*light and fresh food*
prispeva k ugodnemu počutju	*contributes to a feeling of health*
in zdravemu videzu	*and to a healthy appearance*
v obliki mesa	*in a form of meat*
mesni izdelki	*meat products*
jajca	*eggs*
drugi taki proizvodi	*other such products*
tekočine	*liquids*

navadna in mineralna voda	tap and mineral water
razredčeni sokovi	squashes
zeliščni čaji	herbal teas
dodatno zagotavlja	to be assured
dobro delovanje prebavnih organov	good working of digestive organs
upoštevati	take into account
naslednje	the following
ostale	other
ne sodijo med tiste pijače, ki zdravo odžejajo	are not amongst those drinks which refresh you in a healthy manner
bolniki	patients
naj se izogibajo	should avoid
še posebej v vročih dneh	particularly on hot days
posebej nevarne	especially dangerous
kombinacije alkohola, kave in zdravil	combination of alcohol, coffee and medicines

Did you understand?

a What is Simona feeling like? (Explain in Slovene.)
b What does Branka suggest she has? What does she offer to do? (Explain in Slovene.)

Did you know?

1 Če zbolim … *(If I get ill …)*

If you get ill in Slovenia, you will have to go **k zdravniku,** *to see a doctor.* You will find a *clinic,* **ambulanta,** in every town. **Dežurni zdravnik** (*a doctor on duty*) will be available out of working hours; if you cannot go to see him, **bo prišel na dom,** *he will come to your house.*

If you are given a **recept** (*prescription*), you will collect your medicine **v lekarni** (*in a pharmacy*). You will also be able to buy certain medicines over the counter. For urgent needs, certain pharmacies are open during the night.

Citizens of Great Britain are entitled to free emergency medical care in Slovenia.

Recept

The word **recept** has two meanings: it can mean a *cooking recipe* or a *prescription*. The context will indicate the correct meaning.

Ta zdravila dobiš samo na recept.	*This medicine can only be obtained on prescription.*
Kako dobna torta! Ali imaš recept?	*What a good cake! Do you have a recipe?*

2 Naravna zdravilišča *(Natural Health resorts)*

There are a number of natural health resorts in Slovenia. They have been modernized and developed in recent years and provide, apart from medical services, recreational and relaxation facilities.

3 Kaj vas boli? *(What's hurting you?)*

The verb **boleti** means *to hurt*. It is usually used in the third person singular. If you want to ask someone what hurts, say:

Kaj te boli? *or* kaj vas boli? *What hurts you?*

In answer to this question you will be told the part of the body which hurts: You use the accusative case of the noun (usually a name) or a personal pronoun to say who suffers from this pain, for example:

Glava ma boli.	*I have a headache* (lit. *(My) head is hurting me.*)
Grlo ga boli.	*He has a sore throat.* (lit. *(His) throat is hurting him.*)
Zob jo boli.	*She has a toothache.* (lit. *(Her) tooth is hurting her.*)

Here are some more parts of the body, which you can use in the same way:

roka	*arm, hand*	**želodec**	*stomach*
noga	*leg*	**prst**	*finger*
oko	*eye*	**prst na nogi**	*toe*
uho	*ear*	**hrbet**	*back*
koleno	*knee*	**srce**	*heart*

4 More about verbs describing physical feelings

You have already learnt several verbs which describe physical feelings. You also know that if a male is talking, the ending will be different from when a female is talking, for example:

Lačen, –čna sem.	*I'm hungry.*
Žejen, –jna sem.	*I'm thirsty.*
Utrujen, –a sem.	*I'm tired.*
Zaspan, –a sem.	*I'm sleepy.*
Jezen, –zna sem.	*I'm angry.*

Notice that the verb is at the *end* of the sentence in all the examples above. If you negate, and say that you are not . . ., then the verb **nisem** will be at the *beginning* of the sentence, for example:

Nisem lačen.
Nisem žejna.

5 This

The words for '*this*' in Slovene are **ta** for masculine and feminine and **to** for the neuter form, according to the gender of the noun in question:

Ta svinčnik ne piše.	*This pencil doesn't write.*
Ta knjiga je zelo dobra.	*This book is very good.*
To drevo je staro.	*This tree is old.*

When '*this*' is followed by the verb '*to be*', it is always translated by '**to**', regardless of person and number:

To je moj svinčnik.	*This is my pen.*
To je njegova knjiga.	*This is his book.*
To je staro drevo.	*This is an old tree.*

6 This/that

	masculine	feminine	neuter
close by	**ta**	**ta**	**to**
further away	**tisti**	**tista**	**tisto**
very far away	**oni**	**ona**	**ono**

The word for '*this*' is **ta** or **to**, depending on the gender of the noun it refers to. There are two words for '*that*': **tisti** and **oni**. **Tisti** is used for things which are further away, and **oni** for things which are very far away.

7 Reflexive verbs

Verbs followed by **se** or **si** continue to spring up! As you know, they are called *reflexive verbs*. In the sentence *'I wash myself every morning'*, *myself* is the counterpart of **se**. However, there are many more reflexive verbs in Slovene than in English, and you simply have to learn whether they are followed by **se** or **si**. Si is used less frequently than **se**.

vrniti se	*to return*
počutiti se	*to feel*
sprehajati se	*to walk (to promenade)*
izposoditi si	*to borrow*
privoščiti si	*to treat oneself*
ogledati si	*to view*

Se is also used with some impersonal expressions; a few that are commonly used are:

zdi se	*it seems*
(ne) splača se	*it is (not) worth, it pays (does not pay)*
zgodi se	*it happens*

The presence of 'se' can change the meaning, as in these examples:

hvaliti	*to praise*
hvaliti **se**	*to boast*
posoditi	*to lend*
izposoditi **si**	*to borrow*
učiti	*to teach*
učiti **se**	*to learn*

8 More about verbs

Most Slovene verbs can change their meaning by adding a prefix. The change of meaning is sometimes marginal, but at other times considerable. Look at the following example:

- **gledati**   *to look*
  pregledati   *to check*
  zagledati se   *to stare at*
  izgledati   *to appear, to seem*
  pogledati   *to take a look*

- **pisati**   *to write*
  opisati   *to describe*
  prepisati   *to copy*
  pripisati   *to add*
  odpisati   *to write back*
- **stopiti**   *to step*
  izstopiti   *to step out, to get out (of a bus, train, etc.)*
  vstopiti   *to step in, to get into (a bus, train, etc.)*
  prestopiti   *to change (bus, train, etc.)*
  odstopiti   *to resign, to withdraw*

9 Comparing things

When you compare things, you use an adjective or adverb to say that something is better, more expensive, longer, etc. This form is called the *comparative*. If you want to say that something is the best, the most expensive or the longest, you use the *superlative* form.

The comparative form of adjectives is formed by adding –ši, –ji, or –ejši onto the adjective, for example:

lep	*beautiful*	**lepši**	*more beautiful*
drag	*expensive*	**dražji**	*more expensive*
poceni	*cheap*	**cenejši**	*cheaper*

The last letter of the adjective will change when you make a comparative:

> nizek – nižji
> širok – širši
> drag – dražji
> hud – hujši

You can also form a comparative with a helping word, **bolj** (like the English *more*), for example:

rjav	*brown*	bolj rjav	*more brown, browner*
trmast	*stubborn*	bolj trmast	*more stubborn*

You might find this form easier to use. It is not terribly wrong to use it, but it is not good Slovene (it will sound a bit like saying, for example, 'more big').

To **form a superlative**, you simply put **naj–** in front of the comparative, for example: **najnižji, najširši, najdražji**.

When you use the word **bolj**, you put **naj–** in front of **bolj**, for example: **najbolj rjav, najbolj trmast**.

Here are some irregular comparatives and superlatives of adjectives and adverbs:

dober, boljši, najboljši	*good, better, the best*
dobro, bolje, najbolje	*well, better, the best*
veliko, več, največ	*a lot, more, the most*
malo, manj, najmanj	*a little, less, the least*

10 Comparative: 'as' and 'than'

When you compare things you will need to use linking words. When you compare two things which are equal you use **tako . . . kot**, as in:

Miha je **tako** velik **kot** Matjaž. *Miha is as tall as Matjaž.*

When you use the comparative, you use *'than'*:

- **kot** followed by the noun in the nominative *or*
- **od** followed by the noun in the genitive:

Miha je večji **kot** Matjaž *Miha is taller than Matjaž.*
Miha je večji **od** Matjaža.

When you use the superlative, you can use:

- the words **od** or **izmed** followed by the genitive plural, *or*
- **med** followed by the instrumental case:

Miha je največji **od vseh**. *Miha is the tallest of all.*
Miha je največji **izmed vseh**.
Miha je največji **med vsemi**.

▶ Remember!

It is important to be able to describe how you feel, particularly if you are not well. The following expressions will help you:

Ne počutim se dobro.	*I'm not well.*
Glava me boli.	*I have a headache.*
Grlo me boli.	*I have a sore throat.*
Zob me boli.	*I have a toothache.*
Zebe me.	*I feel cold.*
Prehlajen, –a sem	*I have a cold.*
Prehladil, –a sem se.	*I caught a cold.*
Gripo imam.	*I have flu.*
Bolan sem. (m.) Bolna sem. (f.)	*I'm ill.*
Nekaj imam v očesu.	*I have something in my eye.*
Temperaturo imam.	*I have a temperature.*
Kje je najbližja ambulanta?	*Where is the nearest clinic?*
Moram k zdravniku.	*I have to see a doctor.*
Kje je najbližja lekarna?	*Where is the nearest chemist?*

Exercises

1 Your friend says: 'Glava me boli in temperaturo imam.' What is the matter?

▶ 2 How would you say: 'It will be better tomorrow'?

▶ 3 You have arranged to go to the cinema with a friend but you are feeling a bit off colour. Ring him up and say that you are not feeling well. Say that you have a cold.

4 The doctor has prescribed you some medicine. Where do you go to collect it?

5 Here are some parts of the body. Match the Slovene and English equivalents.

a	želodec	1	ear
b	noga	2	heart
c	roka	3	head
d	zob	4	eye
e	oko	5	stomach
f	uho	6	leg
g	glava	7	arm
h	srce	8	tooth

6   Fill in the comparative form of the adjectives given in brackets.

V stari Ljubljani so hiše (stare) kot v novi Ljubljani, ulice so (ozke), in trgovine so (majhne).

7   Tell a person you have met in Slovenia which months in England are usually the coldest, and which the warmest.

8   How would you tell someone which hotel amongst those listed below is the cheapest, and which the most expensive?

Hotel Tram – £746
Hotel Ava – £490
Hotel Lia – £1,129
Hotel Leva – £896

9   Here are some reflexive verbs: **sprehajati se, privoščiti si, zahvaliti se, počutiti se, ogledati si**. Find the appropriate one for each of the sentences below:

a   Tanja mi je kupila darilo. Moram ji telefonirati in —.
b   Že ves teden sem doma, slabo —.
c   Tega — ne morem —, predrago je.
d   — si že — to razstavo?
e   V parku sem videl sosedo. — je s psom.

And something else ...

Darko is taking his driving test. Before he can do his theory test he has to do a first-aid course and pass the test. His friend lent him some notes he took when he was doing the course, and amongst them was the following:

Prva pomoč *(First aid)*

Najprej moramo oceniti ponesrečenca: pokličemo ga, rahlo stresemo in vprašamo, če nas sliši. Če ne odgovori, ga malo uščipnemo, da vidimo, če se odziva na bolečino. Ugotoviti moramo, če diha. Če ne, mu položimo glavo nazaj in dva do trikrat počasi, a močno vpihnemo zrak v njegova odprta usta. Opazujemo, če se prsni koš dvigne. Če je ponesrečenec v avtomobilu, ga ne vlečemo ven, tudi če je pri zavesti. Lahko mu zlomimo hrbtenico. Še to: če je kdo v nezavesti, vendar diha in mu bije srce, ga samo položite na bok in pokličite zdravnika.

oceniti	*to assess*
ponesrečenec	*the casualty*
poklicati	*to call*
rahlo stresti	*to shake slightly*
malo uščipniti	*to pinch a little*
odzivati se	*to react*
na bolečino	*to react to pain*
ugotoviti	*to establish*
dihati	*to breathe*
položiti	*to lay*
nazaj	*backwards*
vpihniti	*to blow in(to)*
zrak	*air*
odprta usta	*opened mouth*
opazovati	*to observe*
prsni koš	*chest*
dvigniti se	*to rise*
vleči ven	*to pull out*
biti pri zavesti	*to be conscious*
zlomiti	*to break*
hrbtenica	*spine*
biti v nezavesti	*to be unconscious*
srce bije	*the heart beats*
položiti na bok	*to lay on side*

13

gremo na izlet!
let's go for a trip!

In this unit you will learn
- how to reserve a hotel room
- how to check into a hotel
- how to buy clothes
- how to use the passive construction
- how the Slovene school system works

▶ Dialogues

Izlet zvlakom *(A trip by train)*

Alenka and Mojca have decided to take advantage of their monthly railway pass and to go for a trip by train to Ptuj, the oldest town in Slovenia. Alenka has found an advertisement which says, 'Oddajamo sobe po ugodnih cenah' (Reasonably priced rooms to let). She rings up the number and Gospa Kotnik answers the telephone.

Alenka	Dobro jutro, Alenka Bogataj pri telefonu. V časopisu sem videla oglas, da oddajate sobe.
Gospa Kotnik	Ja, oddajamo jih. V zasebni hiši, ki ni daleč iz središča mesta.
Alenka	Ali imate proste sobe za ta konec tedna?
Gospa Kotnik	Za koliko oseb pa?
Alenka	Za dve.
Gospa Kotnik	Imamo sobo z dvema posteljama, ampak brez kopalnice. Kopalnica s tušem in straniščem je zraven sobe.
Alenka	Prav. Bi lahko rezervirala to sobo?
Gospa Kotnik	Ja, seveda. Na kakšno ime?
Alenka	Mojca Dolišek in Alenka Bogataj.
Gospa Kotnik	In kdaj boste prišli?
Alenka	V petek popoldne, okoli petih.
Gospa Kotnik	Pričakovali vas bomo torej v petek.

v časopisu	*in a newspaper*
oglas	*advertisement*
oddajati sobe	*to let rooms*
zasebna hiša: v zasebni hiši	*private house: in a private house*
oseba: Za koliko oseb?	*person: For how many people?*
postelja: z dvema posteljama	*bed: with two beds*
tuš: s tušem	*shower: with shower*
stranišče: s straniščem	*toilet: with toilet*
zraven	*next to*
Na kakšno ime?	*In what name?*
pričakovati	*to expect*
torej	*so, thus*

▶ Kaj boš oblekla? *(What will you wear?)*

Alenka and Mojca are deciding what clothes to take with them.

Alenka	Boš vzela s seboj veliko oblek?
Mojca	Ne preveč. Hlače, dve majici in en debel pulover ali jakno. Ob večerih je po navadi hladno.
Alenka	Boš vzela tudi anorak?
Mojca	Ne vem. Misliš, da bo deževalo?
Alenka	Kdo ve? Marca je vreme nezanesljivo.
Mojca	Boš obula čevlje ali superge?
Alenka	Za potovanje bom imela obute superge, čevlje pa bom vzela zraven.
Mojca	Kaj pa za zvečer, če greva ven?
Alenka	Črne hlače in eno bluzo.
Mojca	Dobra ideja!

vzeti s seboj	*to take with one*
za obleči	*to wear*
preveč	*too much*
hlače	*trousers*
majica	*T-shirt*
pulover: debel pulover	*pullover: thick pullover*
jakna	*jacket*
Kdo ve?	*Who knows?*
zanesljiv (-a, -o)	*predictable*
nezanesljiv (-a, -o)	*unpredictable*
čevlji	*shoes*
superge	*trainers*
za potovanje	*for travelling*
imeti obuto	*to wear on the feet*
iti ven: če greva ven	*to go out: if we (two) go out*
črne hlače	*black trousers*
bluza	*blouse*

Mojca and Alenka are taking advantage of the rail card which they bought in order to travel at reduced rates. See the next advertisement in which **Slovenske železnice** (Slovene railways) advertise their discounted fares.

potovanje z vlakom	*travel by train*
dijak	*student (at high school)*
delavec	*worker*
ugodna možnost	*special offer,* lit. *'beneficial possibility'*
vožnja: za vožnjo	*drive, ride: for travelling*
na delo	*to work*
mesečni, –čna, –o	*monthly*
letni, –a, –o	*annual*
dijaška vozovnica	*student* (i.e. high school student) *ticket*
študentska vozovnica	*student ticket*
delavska vozovnica	*worker's ticket*
popust	*discount*
polletna vozovnica	*half-year ticket*
večinoma	*mostly*
mladinska izkaznica	*youth pass*
posebna ugodnost	*special benefit*
znesek	*the price*
poravnati znesek	*to pay the price*
obrok: v enem obroku	*instalment: in one instalment*
namesto	*instead of*

Did you understand?

a What kind of room did Mojca and Alenka book at Mrs Kotnik's house?
b What clothes are they thinking of taking with them?

Did you know?

1 Rezervacija sobe (Reserving a room)

The Slovene tourist board can help you with published prices of hotel accommodation. Apart from hotels, you can stay in private rooms. They can vary from more luxurious to ones with only basic facilities. You can also stay at camping sites, but some of them close during the winter months. If you are going hiking or climbing, you may enjoy staying *on a farm*, **na kmetiji**. You should enquire beforehand whether there are farmhouses which let rooms on the route you are proposing to take.

Z VLAKOM
V ŠOLO IN V SLUŽBO!

Slovenske železnice so za dijake, študente in delavce pripravile dve ugodni možnosti za vožnjo v šolo ali na delo: MESEČNO in LETNO dijaško, študentsko ali delavsko vozovnico.

DIJAŠKE IN ŠTUDENTSKE VOZOVNICE

- tedenska vozovnica — 45 % popusta
- mesečna vozovnica — 60 % popusta
- letna ali polletna vozovnica — 20 % cenejše od mesečne

Dijakom in študentom, ki večinoma potujejo na koncu tedna, priporočamo mladinsko izkaznico, s katero imajo 30 % popusta.

DELAVSKE VOZOVNICE

- tedenska vozovnica — 20 % popusta
- mesečna vozovnica — 25 % popusta
- letna ali polletna vozovnica — 50 % popusta

✳

POSEBNA UGODNOST: Če znesek za letno vozovnico poravnate v enem obroku, plačate samo 8 mesečnih vozovnic namesto 12. V dveh obrokih plačate 8,5 mesečne vozovnice in v treh obrokih 9 mesečnih vozovnic.

 Slovenske železnice

2 Oblačila (Clothes)

The words for some basic items of clothing are:

bluza	blouse	**hlače**	trousers
srajca	shirt	**plašč**	coat
pulover	pullover	**dežni plašč**	raincoat
krilo	skirt		

Note that the word **obleka** can mean *a woman's dress* or *a man's suit*.

Adjectives describing clothing items need appropriate endings. Here are some examples:

Te črne hlače so mi zelo všeč.   *I very much like these black trousers.*

Kje si kupila to lepo krilo?   *Where did you buy this beautiful skirt?*

Letos si moram kupiti nov plašč.   *I must buy a new coat this year.*

3 Obutev (Footwear)

The words for footwear are:

čevlji	shoes	**škornji**	boots
sandali	sandals		

Copati means slippers. You should remember this word, as it is common practice in Slovenia to take your shoes off when you go into your own house, and even if you go to someone's house as a visitor. It is quite offensive not to offer to take off your shoes: you might bring dirt into the house.

4 Katero številko? (What size?)

The word for *size* is **številka**, which, as you know, also means *number*. Clothes and shoes have different sizes in Slovenia from those in Britain and America. You might therefore want to try things on. In this case you ask:

Lahko to pomerim?   *May I try this on?*

You might also hear a shop assistant ask you:

Katero številko želite?   *What size would you like?*

5 Premalo/preveč *(Too little/too much)*

To say that something is *too* ... you simply put the prefix **pre–**
onto the adjective or adverb:

prevelik	*too big*	**prepočasi**	*too slowly*
premajhen	*too small*	**prehitro**	*too fast*

Ta bluza mi je prevelika.   *This blouse is too big for me.*
Plače so prenizke.   *Salaries are too low.*
Premalo denarja imam.   *I have too little money.*

6 Smem ...? *(May I ...?)*

The verb **smeti** means *to be allowed to*. You use it when you
want to be polite. This verb is always followed by an infinitive.
Here are some common expressions using this verb:

Smem ponuditi ...?   *May I offer ...?*
Smem poskusiti to ...?   *May I try this ...?*
Smem telefonirati od tukaj?   *May I make a telephone call
from here?*

7 More on numbers

Numbers are declined in Slovene. 'One' is declined like an
adjective when it modifies a noun, for example:

Imam en**o** sestro in en**ega**   *I have one sister and one
brata.*   *brother.*

For a comprehensive table showing how numbers are declined,
see Appendix 2.

8 More about personal pronouns

As you know, personal pronouns in the nominative case are
hardly used, as the ending of the verb indicates the person. They
are, however, used if you want to express a contrast, or if you
want to emphasize who you are referring to, for example:

Jaz sem šel v kino,   *I went to the cinema and*
ona pa v gledališče.   *she went to the theatre.*
Ti ne smeš piti vina,   *You can't drink wine,*
gripo imaš!   *you have flu!*
Zdaj sem **jaz** na vrsti!   *It is my turn now!*

If you look at the table of personal pronouns in Appendix 3 you will notice that there are sometimes two forms – a longer and a short one. The long form is used for emphasis and after prepositions, but the short form is used more often.

In addition, with prepositions which take the accusative case, you can add the short form onto the preposition. Here are a few examples:

Je to **zame** (za mene)?	*Is this for me?*
Velikokrat mislim **nate** (na tebe).	*I often think of you.*
Prišel bom **pote** (po tebe).	*I'll come to pick you up.*

9 Šolski sistem v Sloveniji *(The school system in Slovenia)*

Children go to **vrtec** (*kindergarten*). When they are 6 years old they go to school. The word for *form* is **razred**. To say what form someone is in you use the verb **hoditi**, which means '*to go regularly, to attend*', for example:

Marija hodi v prvi razred.	*Marija is in the first form.*
Janez hodi v peti razred.	*Janez is in the fifth form.*

You are in **osnovna šola** (*primary school*) for eight years; it is sometimes called **osemletka** (lit. *the eight-year school*) and the word for a pupil in this school is **učenec** (m.)/**učenka** (f.).

When you go to *secondary school*, **srednja šola** (lit. *middle school*) you are no longer **učenec**, but not yet a student: you become a **študent/študentka** at university. The word for a pupil in secondary school, which can last from three to five years, depending on the type of school, is **dijak** (m.) **dijakinja** (f.).

Here are some subjects which every **učenec, dijak** or **študent** will have studied:

matematika	*maths*
fizika	*physics*
kemija	*chemistry*
biologija	*biology*
tuji jeziki	*foreign languages*
zgodovina	*history*
geografija	*geography*

10 Passive

Look at these examples:

Active	*Passive*
Shakespeare wrote many plays.	Many plays *were written* by Shakespeare.
Mark spotted a mistake.	A mistake *was spotted* by Mark.

In the two examples on the left, the subject of the verb performs the action, i.e. *Shakespeare wrote*, *Mark spotted*, whilst in the two examples on the right the subject is the object of the action, i.e. plays *were written by* Shakespeare, a mistake *was spotted* by Mark.

The passive construction is used much less in Slovene than in English. The two examples above could not be expressed in the passive in Slovene, you could only put this message across in the active. You must be careful not to translate ideas which come so naturally to you in English literally into Slovene. Here are a few passive expressions commonly used in English, which would not work in Slovene:

This was given to me.
I was told.
I was promised.

Remember!

If you decide to book a room somewhere in Slovenia, the following phrases will be helpful.

Kje bi lahko prenočili?	*Where could we stay overnight?*
Radi bi bili v mestu/na kmetiji/ob morju/ob jezeru	*We would like to be in town/on a farm/ by the sea/by the lake*
Imate proste sobe?	*Have you any vacancies?*
Koliko stane soba?	*How much is the room?*
Rezerviral sem sobo.	*I reserved a room.*
Ostanem od ... do ...	*I will stay from ... until ...*
Je zajtrk vključen?	*Is breakfast included?*

Exercises

1 Match the Slovene and English equivalents:

a	dežni plašč	1	shoes
b	škornji	2	shirt
c	čevlji	3	trousers
d	hlače	4	boots
e	krilo	5	raincoat
f	srajca	6	shirt

2 You would like a room with a bathroom for two people for one week in a hotel in Slovenia. Ring up and tell them in Slovene what you want.

3 When pottering around in Slovenia you come across the following signs. What do they mean?

a Oddajamo sobe.
b Ugodne cene.
c 20% popusta.
d Plačate lahko v treh obrokih.
e Vstop prost.

4 You have booked a room over the telephone, and the receptionist has asked you to fill in the form which she faxed you to confirm your booking. Can you do so? The vocabulary in the box will help you understand the form.

vpisati	*to fill in*
čitljivo	*legibly*
z modrim ali črnim pisalom	*with blue or blank ink*
Uporabite velike tiskane črke.	*Use block letters.*
vključno	*including*
številka omrežne skupine	*the area code*
na katero	*on which*
vas lahko pokličemo	*we can telephone you*

Prosimo, vpišite svoje ime in naslov - čitljivo, z modrim ali črnim pisalom. Uporabite velike tiskane črke.

Samo za obdelavo podatkov.	(1)=1	(2)=9	(3)-(10)	(11) ☐
URN NO:				

Gospod/Gospa/Gospodična/(prosimo, vpišite) _____

Ime ⌊_____⌋ Priimek ⌊_____⌋

Naslov ⌊_____⌋
⌊_____⌋
Poštna številka ⌊_____⌋

Prosimo, vpišite svoje telefonsko številko (vključno s številko omrežne skupine), na katero Vas lahko pokličemo.

čez dan ⌊_____⌋ zvečer ⌊_____⌋

5 You have booked a room for the weekend and are asked when you will arrive. Say: 'On Friday evening at about 7 o'clock'.

6 You are in a restaurant and want to use the toilet. Ask the waitress where it is.

7 Tell your friend who is coming to your place for a meal that you will expect her on Saturday at about six o'clock.

8 It is summer. You are going to the seaside for a week's holiday. Make a list of the things you will take with you.

9 You are buying a coffee-percolator. The shop assistant says: '**Znesek lahko poravnate v treh obrokih.**' What did she mean?

10 a It is a hot summer's day. Say: 'It is too hot today.'
 b You have been asked to go to Russia for a week in February. Say: 'In February it is too cold in Russia.'
 c You have tried on a pullover you liked, and as you come out of the changing-room the shop assistant asks you whether it was OK. Tell her that it is too big.
 d A friend of yours had his driving licence confiscated. Another friend asks you whether you know why. Tell her that your friend had been driving too fast.

11 Describe what you are wearing.

And something else ...

An Englishman called James Roberts is booking into a hotel.

James	Dober večer.
Receptorka	Dober večer. elite, prosim?
James	Prejšnji teden sem rezerviral sobo. Pravzaprav, moja tajnica je rezervirala sobo zame.
Receptorka	Ja, kako se pišete?
James	Roberts
Receptorka	Samo trenutek. Ja, imamo sobo za vas. Enoposteljna soba s kopalnico in majhnim balkonom je. V petem nadstropju je, v hotelu je dvigalo.
James	Prav.
Receptorka	Številka sobe je 532. Izvolite ključ. Poklicala bom postrežčka, on bo odnesel vašo prtljago.
James	Je restavracija še odprta?
Receptorka	Ne več, ampak če želite kaj pojesti, v sobi je jedilni list za postrežbo v sobo.

James   Prav, pogledal bom. In še nekaj: kdaj je zjutraj zajtrk?
Receptorka Od sedmih do desetih. Če želite, vam lahko prinesemo tudi zajtrk v sobo.
James   Hvala za enkrat.

rezervirati sobo	*to reserve a room*
pravzaprav	*actually, that is to say*
moja tajnica	*my secretary*
zame	*for me*
Kako se pišete?	*What is your surname?*
enoposteljna soba	*a single room*
v petem nadstropju	*on the fifth floor*
dvigalo	*lift*
ključ	*key*
postrežček	*porter*
nesti: odnesti	*to carry: to take away*
prtljaga	*luggage*
če želite kaj pojesti	*if you would like something to eat*
postrežba v sobo	*room service*
gledati: pogledati	*to look: to take a look*

Unit 1

Dialogues 1 **a** čaj (*b*) denarnica 2 (1) a (2) b (3) c

Exercises 1 **a** Dobro jutro. **b** Prosim? **c** Dober večer. **d** Prosim.
e Izvolite! **f** Hvala. **g** Kako gre? **h** Najlepša hvala **i** Ni za kaj
2 jutro; dobro; kako; dobro 3 Refer to '**prosim**' on p. 7.
4 **a** Oprostite. **b** Oprosti. 5 **a** denarnica **b** dan **c** mleko **d** denar
e hvala **f** prosim **g** sin **h** ime **i** čaj **j** mož 6 Dober dan. Zelo dobro,
hvala. Ja, to je moj sin. Ime mi je Matjaž. Me veseli.

Unit 2

Dialogues a Tanja je učiteljica. **b** Caroline je na dopustu. **c** Klaus je
računovodja. Dela na banki. **d** Suzan je v Sloveniji že eno leto.
e David razume skoraj vse ampak govori slabo.

Exercises 1 **a** govori **b** razume **c** živi **d** je **e** ima **f** dela 2 **a** Od kod
ste? **b** Ali govorite angleško? **c** Kaj ste po poklicu? **d** Kje stanujete?
3 **a** Janet je Angležinja. **b** Christin je Avstrijka. **c** Boris je Rus.
d Jean-Paul je Francoz. **e** Henry je Anglež. **f** Johann je Nemec.
4 **a** Ne delam na banki. **b** Nataša ne stanuje v Berlinu. **c** Moja
mama ne govori dobro slovensko. **d** Ne razumem francosko.
e Mitja ni po poklicu kuhar. 5 **a** zdravnik **b** jezik **c** družina
d prodajalec **e** igralka **f** pevka **g** banka **h** učitelj **i** zakaj **j** kje
6 Albanija, Madžarska, Francija, Finska, Švica, Avstralija, Rusija,
Nemčija, Romunija, Irska, Anglija, Indija, Italija, Kanada
7 **a** Duncan je Škot. **b** Po poklicu je kuhar. **c** Dela v hotelu. 8 Ime
mi je (*say your name*). (*Say your nationality*) sem. Po poklicu sem
(*say your profession*). Delam v (*say the place where you work*).
9 Razumem malo slovensko, ampak ne govorim dobro. 10 Vlado:
Ali stanujete v Ljubljani? Vlado: Od kod ste? Vlado: Dobro
govorite slovensko. Vlado: Razumem veliko ampak govorim slabo.

11 Portugalska, Slovenija, Italija, Avstrija, Španija, Švica, Norveška, Belgija, Poljska, Bolgarija, Švedska, Danska, Nemčija, Turčija, Velika Britanija, Češka, Francija, Madžarska, Irska, Severna Irska, Slovaška, Romunija, Grčija, Nizozemska, Finska.

Unit 3

Dialogues **a** On Friday. **b** Return. **c** In the morning and in the evening.

Exercises **1** sobota **2** ponedeljek, torek, sreda, četrtek, petek, sobota, nedelja **3** **a** weekend **b** a house in the country **4** petinsedemdeset **5** on Thursday afternoon **6** s kreditno kartico **7** z avtom **8** ljubezen **9** februarja in avgusta **10** Refer to p. 160–161, where these numbers are listed. **11** **a** neuter **b** neuter **c** masculine **d** masculine **e** masculine **f** feminine **g** masculine **h** feminine **12** **a** aeroplane **b** airport **c** train **d** bus, coach **e** Tuesday **f** Sunday **g** discount **h** ticket

Unit 4

Dialogues **a** He has to go straight on along the main road and turn left by the traffic lights, which will bring him to **Čopova ulica**. At the end of this street there is Tromostovje. **b** There are a lot of pubs by the river. **c** Ljubljanica.

Exercises **1** **a** Pojdite naravnost in pri semaforju zavijte na desno. **b** Is it far? **c** Pet minut hoje je. **2** Žal mi je, ne vem. Nisem iz Ljubljane. **3** Oprostite, ne govorim dobro slovensko. Ne, nisem na dopustu. Tukaj sem poslovno. Delam na banki. Ja, všeč mi je. **4** **b** V torek moram iti na sestanek ob desetih dopoldne. **c** V sredo moram iti na pošto. **d** V četrtek moram kupiti karte za v kino. **e** V petek moram telefonirati Sonji. **5** Prišel sem peš. **6** Lahko tukaj kadim? Ne kadimo v pisarni. **7** Vozite previdno! **8** **a** njegov **b** njen **c** moja **d** njihova **e** njena **f** naše **g** tvoje *or* vaše **h** njihov

Unit 5

Dialogues **a** 0044 **b** poštni nabiralnik **c** Some sort of document which has a photograph.

Exercises **1** telefonska govorilnica **2** **rumena** (It is in the feminine form – all the other colours are in the masculine form.) **3** Oprostite, kje je najbližja banka? **4** Rad bi zamenjal petdeset angleških funtov. **5** znamka, razglednica **6** priporočeno **7** **a** svetlo rjav **b** belo vino **c** rdeče vino **d** rumen poštni nabiralnik **e** temno moder avto **f** bela kuverta **8** bela – črna nov – star dobro – slabo povratna –

enosmerna svetlo – temno **9** Where he can change travellers'
cheques. **10 a** enajsti december **b** šestindvajseti februar
c enaintrideseti avgust **d** sedmi april **11 a** Kupiti moram eno
razglednico in znamko. **b** Ali imaš pri sebi študentsko izkaznico?
c Tukaj imajo dobro kavo.

Unit 6

Dialogues a Simon **b** Today at 7.00 p.m. **c** He went to the cinema
with Irena.

Exercises 1 Banka je odprta od ponedeljka do petka od osmih zjutraj
do šestih zvečer. V soboto je odprta od osmih zjutraj do enih.
V nedeljo je banka zaprta. **2** At eight in the evening. **3** dan
4 Deževalo je. **5 a** Ura je sedem. *or* Ura je devetnajst. **b** Ura je štiri
in petnajst minut. *or* Ura je šestnajst in petnajst minut. **c** Ura je šest in
trideset minut. *or* Ura je osemnajst in trideset minut. **d** Ura je osem in
petinštirideset minut. *or* Ura je dvajset in pentinštirideset minut.
6 a Trikrat. **b** Ne, redko *or* malokrat. **c** Ja, dvakrat, ampak ni je bilo
doma. **7** Včeraj dopoldne ob desetih. **8 a** sem šel **b** sem prišel **c** Bil
sem **9** last month **10** od osmih zjutraj do sedmih zvečer

Unit 7

Dialogues a For her mother: a CD. For her sister: something at the
market. **b** Sara ordered **jabolčni zavitek** (*apple strudel*); Irena ordered
sirove palačinke (*cheese pancakes*).

Exercises 1 a belo kavo **b** čaj z mlekom **c** belo vino **2 a** Rad – a
poslušam klasično glasbo. **b** Rad – a potujem. **c** Rad – a gledam
televizijo. **3** Kako se počutiš? **4 a** V ponedeljek moram telefonirati
ženi. **b** V sredo moram napisati kratko pismo moji tajnici. **c** V petek
moram kupiti darilo za ženo. **5** Rad – a imam (for those you *like*).
Raje imam (for those you *prefer*). Najraje imam (for those you *like
most*). All nouns will be in the accusative case as follows: pop glasbo,
klasično glasbo, jazz, plesno glasbo, folklorno glasbo, rock and roll
6 Ne, hvala, nisem lačen – čna. **7** Za enkrat ne bom nič, hvala.
Kasneje bom naročil – a kavo. **8** Don't worry! **9 a** Danes zvečer
bom . . . **b** Jutri bom . . . **c** Naslednji teden bom . . . **d** Naslednje leto
bom . . .

Unit 8

Dialogues a A loaf of brown bread, a loaf of white bread and 4
bread rolls. **b** Ten pork chops (he doesn't want them to be fat), a kilo
of beef, and a kilo of pork mince.

Exercises 1 a – 8 b –7 c – 5 d – 2 e – 1 f – 3 g – 6 h – 4 2 a en kilogram jabolk b pol litra rdečega vina c en liter mleka d pol kilograma mletega mesa 3 a Bi še kaj drugega? b To bi bilo vse, hvala. 4 a knjigarna b mesnica c pekarna d čistilnica 5 a Bi kavo? b Bi raje čaj? c Bi sok? d Bi kozarec vina? 6 Kdo je na vrsti? 7 Hleb črnega in štruco belega, prosim. 8 raca 9 a rdečega vina b meseca c tedna d skodelica kave

Unit 9

Dialogues a There are a reception room, dining-room and kitchen downstairs, and three bedrooms and a bathroom upstairs. **b** A dishwasher was delivered instead of a washing machine.

Exercises 1 a – 3 b – 5 c – 1 d – 2 e – 4 2 In the kitchen. 3 Kako veliko je tvoje/vaše stanovanje? 4 Petinšestdeset kvadratnih metrov. 5 živimo v štirisobni vrstni hiši. Spodaj so kuhinja, dnevna soba in jedilnica, zgoraj pa štiri spalnice in kopalnica. 6 Hvala za povabilo! 7 Kako dolgo že stanuješ tukaj? 8 He has moved house. 9 Rad bi vas povabil na kosilo./Želite priti na kosilo? 10 a kupili b zapri c pospravljam d kupuješ e izvaža/izvozila

Unit 10

Dialogues Nadja ordered **ocvrte sardine** (*fried sardines*) as a starter, aubergine salad as the main course, and a small glass of beer. Tatjana ordered a cold tomato soup as a starter, aubergine salad as the main course, and a glass of white wine.

Exercises 1 Mizo za dva, prosim. 2 Here is the menu. 3 pijača 4 a kozarec rdečega vina b kozarec belega vina c eno veliko pivo d eno malo pivo e eno belo kavo z sladkorjem f en sadni sok 5 **Rad – a imam –** and list the ones you like (they will be in the accusative case). **Nimam rad –** and list the ones you don't like (they will be in the genitive case). 6 Mi lahko kaj priporočate? 7 a – 3 b – 6 c – 4 d – 5 e – 7 f – 1 g – 2 8 Ne, hvala, ampak bilo je zelo dobro.

Unit 11

Dialogues They will take the hiking gear with them because in spring the weather can be changeable. They will cycle to the mountain hut Tram and stay there for the night. From there they will walk covering approximately 25 km a day. Igor has a good guide book and a detailed map. He will also find out what the weather forecast is for the next few days.

Exercises 1 Včasih grem v službo s kolesom in včasih grem peš.
2 Kakšno je spomladi vreme v Sloveniji? **3** It is cloudy and quite
cold. **4 a** – 4 **b** – 5 **c** – 8 **d** – 1 **e** – 7 **f** – 2 **g** – 3 **h** – 6 **5** northwest
6 Portugalska leži zahodno od Španije. **7** jesenski (It is an adjective.)
8 Pozimi je –, spomladi je –, poleti je –, v jeseni je – **9** Let's go for a
walk in the park. **10** Manja še ni gotova. **11** – Rad bi najel gorsko
kolo. – Za štiri dni. Koliko stane na dan? – Mi lahko pokažete
kolesa? – Kako daleč je do mesta?

Unit 12

Dialogues a Simona se slabo počuti. Glava jo boli, kašlja in zelo jo
zebe. Zelo je utrujena in zaspana. **b** Branka meni, da ima gripo in da
bo čez par dni bolje.

Exercises 1 He or she has a headache and a temperature. **2** Jutri bo
bolje. **3** Ne počutim se dobro, prehladil – a sem se. **4** V
lekarno. **5** **a** – 5 **b** – 6 **c** – 7 **d** – 8 **e** – 4 **f** – 1 **g** – 3 **h** – 2 **6**
starejše, ožje, manjše **7** Najhladnejši so . . . (list the months) in
najtoplejši so . . . (list the months). **8** Najcenejši je Hotel Ava in
najdražji je Hotel Lia. **9 a** se zahvaliti **b** se počutim **c** si ne morem
privoščiti **d** si že ogledal **e** sprehajala se

Unit 13

Dialogues a They booked a room with two beds but no bathroom.
b Not many; Mojca will take a pair of trousers, two T-shirts, and a
thick pullover or a jacket. She will wear trainers for travelling and
take a pair of shoes with her. In case they go out in the evening she
will take a pair of black trousers and a blouse.

Exercises 1 a – 5 **b** – 4 **c** – 1 **d** – 3 **e** – 6 **f** – 2 **2** Rad bi rezerviral
sobo s kopalnico za dve osebi za en teden. **3 a** Rooms to let **b**
Reduced (*lit.* 'beneficial' prices) **c** 20% discount **d** You can pay in
three instalments **e** Entrance free of charge **4** Fill in the form with
your personal details. **5** V petek zvečer okoli sedmih. **6** Oprostite,
kje je stranišče? **7** Pričakoval te bom v soboto okoli šestih. **8** Use
the glossary at the back to help you with vocabulary. **9** You can pay
in three instalments. **10 a** Danes je prevroče. **b** Februarja je v Rusiji
premrzlo. **c** Prevelik je. **d** Prehitro je vozil.

appendices

The following appendices will help you when you are not certain about the ending of a particular noun or adjective in a particular case.

Appendix 1: Slovene nouns

Slovene nouns are characterized by *gender*, *number* and *case*. There are:

- three genders: *masculine*, *feminine* and *neuter*
- three numbers: *singular*, *dual* and *plural*
- six cases: *nominative*, *genitive*, *dative*, *accusative*, *locative* and *instrumental*

Nouns, pronouns, adjectives and numerals are declined, which means that they change their form from one case to another, depending on their function in a given sentence.

Declensions

Slovene nouns are divided into four groups called *declensions*.

First declension: *feminine nouns ending in –a*
Second declension: *feminine nouns ending in a consonant*
Third declension: *masculine nouns*
Fourth declension: *neuter nouns*

Declining feminine nouns ending in –a with an adjective modifying them

Singular

Nominative:	velika hiša	široka cesta	nova obleka
Genitive:	velike hiše	široke ceste	nove obleke
Dative:	veliki hiši	široki cesti	novi obleki
Accusative:	veliko hišo	široko cesto	novo obleko
Locative:	v veliki hiši	pri široki cesti	v novi obleki
Instrumental:	z veliko hišo	s široko cesto	z novo obleko

Dual

Nominative:	veliki hiši	široki cesti	novi obleki
Genitive:	velikih hiš	širokih cest	novih oblek
Dative:	velikima hišama	širokima cestama	novima oblekama
Accusative:	veliki hiši	široki cesti	novi obleki
Locative:	v velikih hišah	pri širokih cestah	v novih oblekah
Instrumental:	z velikima hišama	s širokima cestama	z novima oblekama

Plural

Nominative:	velike hiše	široke ceste	nove obleke
Genitive:	velikih hiš	širokih cest	novih oblek
Dative:	velikim hišam	širokim cestam	novim oblekam
Accusative:	velike hiše	široke ceste	nove obleke
Locative:	v velikih hišah	pri širokih cestah	v novih oblekah
Instrumental:	z velikimi hišami	s širokimi cestami	z novimi oblekami

velika hiša (*big house*); široka cesta (*wide road*); nova obleka (*new dress*)

Declining feminine nouns ending in a consonant

Singular

Nominative:	pesem	malenkost	stvar	prireditev
Genitive:	pesmi	malenkosti	stvari	prireditve
Dative:	pesmi	malenkosti	stvari	prireditvi
Accusative:	pesem	malenkost	stvar	prireditev
Locative:	v pesmi	o malenkosti	o stvari	na prireditvi
Instrumental:	s pesmijo	z malenkostjo	s stvarjo	s prireditvijo

Dual

Nominative:	pesmi	malenkosti	stvari	prireditvi
Genitive:	pesmi	malenkosti	stvari	prireditev
Dative:	pesm**ima**	malenkost**ma/ima**	stvar**ema**	prireditv**ama**
Accusative:	pesmi	malenkosti	stvari	prireditvi
Locative:	v pesm**ih**	o malenkost**ih**	o stvar**eh**	na prireditv**ah**
Instrumental:	s pesm**ima**	z malenkost**ma/ima**	s stvar**ema**	s prireditv**ama**

Plural

Nominative:	pesmi	malenkosti	stvari	prireditve
Genitive:	pesmi	malenkosti	stvari	prireditev
Dative:	pesm**im**	malenkost**im**	stvar**em**	prireditv**am**
Accusative:	pesmi	malenkosti	stvari	prireditve
Locative:	v pesm**ih**	o malenkost**ih**	o stvar**eh**	na prireditv**ah**
Instrumental:	s pesm**imi**	z malenkost**mi**	s stvar**mi**	s prireditv**ami**

pesem (*song*); **malenkost** (*a mere trifle*); **stvar** (*thing*); **prireditev** (*show*)

Note: The adjectives modifying feminine nouns ending in a consonant are declined in the same way as those modifying feminine nouns ending in **–a**.

Declining masculine nouns with an adjective modifying them

Singular

Nom:	današnji časopis	nov dežnik	dober prijatelj
Gen:	današnj**ega** časopis**a**	nov**ega** dežnik**a**	dob**rega** prijatelj**a**
Dat:	današnj**emu** časopis**u**	nov**emu** dežnik**u**	dob**remu** prijatelj**u**
Acc:	današnji časopis	nov dežnik	dob**rega** prijatelj**a**
Loc:	v današnj**em** časopis**u**	o nov**em** dežnik**u**	pri dob**rem** prijatelj**u**
Instr:	z današnj**im** časopis**om**	z nov**im** dežnik**om**	z dob**rim** prijatelj**em**

Dual

Nom:	današnja časopisa	nova dežnika	dobra prijatelja
Gen:	današnj**ih** časopis**ov**	nov**ih** dežnik**ov**	dob**rih** prijatelj**ev**
Dat:	današnj**ima** časopis**oma**	nov**ima** dežnik**oma**	dob**rima** prijatelj**ema**
Acc:	današnja časopisa	nova dežnika	dobra prijatelja
Loc:	v današnj**ih** časopis**ih**	o nov**ih** dežnik**ih**	pri dob**rih** prijatelj**ih**
Instr:	z današnj**ima** časopis**oma**	z nov**ima** dežnik**oma**	z dob**rima** prijatelj**ema**

Plural

Nom:	današnji časopisi	novi dežniki	dobri prijatelji
Gen:	današnjih časopisov	novih dežnikov	dobrih prijateljev
Dat:	današnjim časopisom	novim dežnikom	dobrim prijateljem
Acc:	današnje časopise	nove dežnike	dobre prijatelje
Loc:	v današnjih časopisih	o novih dežnikih	pri dobrih prijateljih
Instr:	z današnjimi časopisi	z novimi dežniki	z dobrimi prijatelji

Note: There are some masculine nouns which end in –a. They are conjugated like feminine nouns ending in –a. Among them are: **pismonoša** (*postman*), **računovodja** (*accountant*), some male names (e.g. **Aljoša, Mitja**).

današnji časopis (*today's newspaper*); **nov dežnik** (*new umbrella*); **dober prijatelj** (*good friend* (male))

Declining neuter nouns with an adjective modifying them

Singular

Nominative:	veliko mesto	lepo stanovanje	tuje ime
Genitive:	velikega mesta	lepega stanovanja	tujega imena
Dative:	velikemu mestu	lepemu stanovanju	tujemu imenu
Accusative:	veliko mesto	lepo stanovanje	tuje ime
Locative:	pri velikem mestu	pri lepem stanovanju	o tujem imenu
Instrumental:	z velikim mestom	z lepim stanovanjem	s tujim imenom

Dual

Nominative:	veliki mesti	lepi stanovanji	tuji imeni
Genitive:	velikih mest	lepih stanovanj	tujih imen
Dative:	velikima mestoma	lepima stanovanjema	tujima imenoma
Accusative:	veliki mesti	lepi stanovanji	tuji imeni
Locative:	pri velikih mestih	pri lepih stanovanjih	pri tujih imenih
Instrumental:	z velikima mestoma	z lepima stanovanjema	s tujima imenoma

Plural

Nominative:	velika mesta	lepa stanovanja	tuja imena
Genitive:	velikih mest	lepih stanovanj	tujih imen
Dative:	velikim mestom	lepim stanovanjem	tujim imenom
Accusative:	velika mesta	lepa stanovanja	tuja imena
Locative:	pri velikih mestih	pri lepih stanovanjih	pri tujih imenih
Instrumental:	z velikimi mesti	z lepimi stanovanji	s tujimi imeni

veliko mesto (*large town*); lepo stanovanje (*beautiful flat*); tuje ime (*foreign name*)

Declining plural nouns with an adjective modifying them

Nominative:	umazana tla	odprta vrata	prijetni ljudje
Genitive:	umazanih tal	odprtih vrat	prijetnih ljudi
Dative:	umazanim tlom	odprtim vratom	prijetnim ljudem
Accusative:	umazana tla	odprta vrata	prijetne ljudi
Locative:	na umazanih tleh	pri odprtih vratih	o prijetnih ljudeh
Instrumental:	z umazanimi tlemi/tli	z odprtimi vrati	s prijetnimi ljudmi

umazana tla (*dirty floor*); odprta vrata (*open door*); prijetni ljudje (*pleasant people*)

Some other plural nouns are:

usta (*mouth*); pljuča (*lungs*); jetra (*liver*); starši (*parents*); očala (*spectacles*)

Appendix 2: Declining numbers

one

	m.	*f.*	*n.*
Nominative:	eden/en	ena	eno
Genitive:	enega	ene	enega
Dative:	enemu	eni	enemu
Accusative:	enega	eno	eno
Locative:	pri enem	pri eni	pri enim
Instrumental:	z enim	z eno	z enim

two

	m.	f.	n.
Nominative:	dva	dve	dve
Genitive:	dveh	dveh	dveh
Dative:	dvema	dvema	dvema
Accusative:	dva	dve	dve
Locative:	pri dveh	pri dveh	pri dveh
Instrumental:	z dvema	z dvema	z dvema

three

	m.	f.	n.
Nominative:	trije	tri	tri
Genitive:	treh	treh	treh
Dative:	trem	trem	trem
Accusative:	tri	tri	tri
Locative:	pri treh	pri treh	pri treh
Instrumental:	s tremi	s tremi	s tremi

four

	m.	f.	n.
Nominative:	štirje	štiri	štiri
Genitive:	štirih	štirih	štirih
Dative:	štirim	štirim	štirim
Accusative:	štiri	štiri	štiri
Locative:	pri štirih	pri štirih	pri štirih
Instrumental:	s štirimi	s štirimi	s štirimi

The numbers from five onwards are the same for all three genders, and follow this pattern:

five	six	seven	eight	nine	ten
pet	šest	sedem	osem	devet	deset
petih	šestih	sedmih	osmih	devetih	desetih
petim	šestim	sedmim	osmim	devetim	desetim
pet	šest	sedem	osem	devet	deset
pri petih	pri šestih	pri sedmih	pri osmih	pri devetih	pri desetih
s petimi	s šestimi	s sedmimi	z osmimi	z devetimi	z desetimi

Appendix 3: Declining personal pronouns

Nom.	Gen.	Dat.	Acc.	Loc.	Instr.
Singular					
jaz	mene/me	meni/mi	mene/me	pri meni	z menoj
ti	tebe/te	tebi/ti	tebe/te	pri tebi	s teboj
on	njega/ga	njemu/mu	njega/ga	pri njem	z njim
ona	nje/je	njej/ji	njo/jo	pri njej	z njo
ono	njega/ga	njemu/mu	njega/ga	pri njem	z njim
Dual					
midva	naju	nama	naju	pri nama	z nama
vidva	vaju	vama	vaju	pri vaju	z vama
				vama	
onadva	njiju	njima/jima	njiju	pri njiju	z njima
	nju, njih			njima	
Plural					
mi	nas	nam	nas	pri nas	z nami
vi	vas	vam	vas	pri vas	z vami
oni	njih/jih	njim/jim	njih/jih	pri njih	z njimi

adjective An adjective is a word used to qualify or describe a noun or pronoun, e.g. My brother is **tall**. *Moj brat je **velik**.* My mother is **young**. *Moja mama je **mlada**.*

adverb Adverbs are used to qualify or modify an adjective or a verb, e.g. She is **very** young. *Ona je **zelo** mlada.* Ann sings **well**. *Ana **dobro** poje.*

agreement Agreement is when words which are used together have the same grammatical number, gender and case.

case Cases are indicated by changes made to nouns, adjectives, pronouns and numerals. There are six cases in Slovene: nominative, genitive, dative, accusative, locative and instrumental. Cases tell the function of a noun in a sentence.

comparative When making comparisons we need the comparative form of the adjective. In English this is done by adding -er to the adjective or by putting **more** in front. This table is **higher** than that one. *Ta miza je **višja** kot ona.* This house is **more** expensive. *Ta hiša je **bolj** draga.*

conditional This is the form of the verb to show that an event might have happened or might yet take place.

dual See **singular**.

enclitics Slovene has two forms for personal pronouns in cases other than the nominative. The shorter form of these alternatives is called the 'enclitic'.

gender In Slovene all nouns have a gender which is masculine, feminine or neuter. Sometimes the grammatical gender of a noun may tell you if the word refers to a male or a female being but it is not primarily a biological reference. The word **chair** *stol* is masculine, while **table** *miza* is feminine and **sea** *morje* is neuter. Adjectives which are used to describe nouns must agree with the gender of the noun and change accordingly.

imperative The imperative is the form of the verb used to give directions, instructions, orders or commands.

infinitive The infinitive is the basic form of the verb. In English the infinitive is formed from two words (**to write**), while in Slovene it is one word which ends in either **-ti** (*pisati* – **to write**) or **-či** (*peči* – **to bake**).

noun Nouns are words which refer to things and people, e.g. **room** *soba*, **person** *človek*.

number Number is the term used to indicate whether words are singular or plural.

person Person is a term which refers to the separate parts of a verb. Verbs in Slovene have nine persons: three in singular, three in dual and three in plural, and endings of verbs change accordingly.

plural See **singular**.

possessive adjectives Possessive adjectives such as **my** and **mine** indicate who possesses what in a sentence. This is **my** car. That car is **yours**. *To je **moj** avto. Tisti avto je **tvoj**.*

preposition Prepositions are words which generally show relationships between people or things, e.g. Helen is **in** the room. *Helena je **v** sobi.*

pronouns Pronouns are often used to substitute nouns which have usually been mentioned once already. This is my husband. *He is working in the garden.* To je moj mož. *On dela na vrtu.* Such pronouns as **I** *jaz*, **he** *on* are called personal pronouns and are often omitted in Slovene because the ending of the verb indicates the person, e.g. This is my husband. He is working in the garden. *To je moj mož. Dela na vrtu.*

reflexive verb These are constructions in which the word *se*, meaning **oneself**, accompanies the verb.

singular The terms singular, dual and plural are used to contrast between one, two or more persons or things, e.g. **one book / two books / three books**: *ena knjiga / dve knjigi / tri knjige*.

superlative The superlative part of the adjective is formed in English by adding **-est** to the adjective or by using **most**. This shirt is the **cheapest** of all. *Ta srajca je od vseh **najcenejša**.* This bag is the **most** expensive. *Ta torba je **najbolj** draga.*

tense Tense indicates the time when the action of the verb in a sentence takes place.

verb Verbs usually indicate the action of a sentence, e.g. **He is writing a letter.** *On piše pismo.*

verbal aspect The aspect of a verb tells you more about the quality of the action in a sentence. It tells you if the action was or will be completed, if the action took place or will take place on more than one occasion, if the action was or will be in process but not completed. Slovene has an imperfective aspect (for unfinished or regular actions, e.g. **to write** *pisati*) and a perfective aspect (for completed actions, e.g. **to write** *napisati*). **He wrote to his mother every day.** *Vsak dan je pisal svoji materi.* **Yesterday he wrote a short letter.** *Včeraj je napisal kratko pismo.*

advokat *lawyer; solicitor*
aktovka *briefcase*
ali *or*; can also indicate a question
Američan, –ka(f.) *American*
Amerika *America*
ampak *but*
ananas *pineapple*
Anglež, –inja (f.) *Englishman, –woman*
Anglija *England*
apartma *apartment*
aperitiv *aperitif*
artičoka *artichoke*
aspirin *aspirin*
ata *father*
Avstralija *Australia*
avto *car*
avtobus *bus; coach*
avtobusna postaja *bus-station, bus-stop*
avtocesta *motorway*
avtomatičen, –čna, –o *automatic*
avtor, –ica (f.) *author*

balkon *balcony*
banana *banana*
banka *bank*
bančni račun *bank account*
bar *bar* (pub)
barva *colour*
baterija *battery*

bel, –a, –o *white*
beležka *note-pad*
beljak *egg-white*
beluš *asparagus*
bencin *petrol*
beseda *word*
bife *buffet, snack bar*
blagajna *cash desk, till*
blažilec *shock absorber*
bliskanje *lightning*
blizu *near*
bluza *blouse*
Bog *God*
bogat, –a, –o *rich*
bolan, –a, –o *sick, ill*
bolečina *pain*
boleti *ache, hurt*
bolje (kot) *better* (than)
bolnišnica *hospital*
bombaž *cotton*
božič *Christmas*
brat *brother*
brati *read*
breskev *peach*
brez *without*
brezplačen, –čna, –o *free of charge*
brisača *towel*
Britanija *Britain*
briti *shave* (vb.)
brivec *barber*
brošura *brochure*
budilka *alarm clock*

carina *customs*
cel, –a, –o *whole; all; total*
cena *cost, charge, price*
ceneje *cheaper*
cenik *price list*
cerkev *church*
cesta *street; road, way*
cigara *cigar*
cigarete *cigarettes*
copati *slippers*
cvetača *cauliflower*
čaj *tea*
čaj z limono *lemon tea*
čaj z mlekom *tea with milk*
čajnik *teapot*
čakalnica *waiting-room*
čakati (na) *wait (for)*
čas *time*
časopis *newspaper*
če *if*
čebela *bee*
čebula *onion*
češnja *cherry*
ček *cheque*
čekovna knjižica *cheque book*
česen *garlic*
čestitke *congratulations*
čevelj *shoe*
čez *across; after (time)*
čigav, –a, –o *whose*
čipka *lace*
čist, –a, –o *clean* (adj.)
čistilnica *dry cleaner's*
čistiti *clean* (vb.)
član *member*
članek *article*
človek *person*
čokolada *chocolate*
čoln *boat*
čolnarna *boat-house*
črka *letter of alphabet*
črn, –a, –o *black*

da *yes; that* (conj.)
daleč *far*
daljnogled *binoculars*
dan *day*
danes *today*
darilo *present; gift*

dati *give*
datum *date*
davek *tax*
debel, –a, –o *fat* (person);
  thick (book)
dekle *girl*
del *part*
delati *work* (vb.); *do* (vb.)
delikatese *delicatessen*
delo *work*
denar *money*
denarnica *purse; wallet*
dež *rain* (n.)
dežela *country*
dežni plašč *raincoat*
dežnik *umbrella*
dežuje *raining: it's raining*
dijeta *diet*
direktor *manager*
dneven, –vna, –o *daily*
dnevna soba *living-room;
  lounge*
do *till* (conj.)
dober, –bra, –o *good*
dobiti *get (obtain)*
dobro *well*
dobrodošli! *welcome!*
dodatek *supplement*
dodati *add* (vb.)
dogovor *agreement*
dokumenti *documents*
dol *down*
dolar *dollar*
dolg *debt* (n.)
dolg, –a, –o *long* (adj.)
dolgočasen, –sna, –o *boring*
dolgovati *owe*
dolina *valley*
dolžina *length*
dom *home*
doma *at home*
domotožje *homesick*
dopust *holiday*
dovoliti *let; allow; permit*
dovolj *enough*
drag, –a, –o *dear; expensive*
drevo *tree*
driska *diarrhoea*
drobiž *money; change* (n.)

drugačen, –čna, –o *different*
drugi, –a, –o *other; second*
družina *family*
država *country*
državljanstvo *nationality*
duhovnik *priest*
dvakrat *twice*
dvigalo *lift*
dvom *doubt* (n.)
dvomiti *doubt* (vb.)

eden; en *one*
električar *electrician*
električen, –čna, –o *electric*
elektrika *electricity*
enkrat *once*
enolončnica *stew*

fant *boy; boyfriend*
fen *hairdryer*
festival *festival*
film *film; also roll for camera*
firma *company; firm*
fižol *beans*
fotoaparat *camera*
fotografija *photograph*
fotografirati *to take photographs*
fotokopirati *photocopy* (vb.)
Francija *France*
Francoz-inja *Frenchman, –woman*
frizer *hairdresser*
funt *English pound*

galerija *gallery*
garaža *garage*
garderoba *cloakroom; left-luggage office*
gasilci *fire brigade*
glas *voice*
glasba *music*
glasen, –sna, –o *loud*
glava *head*
glavni, –vna, –o *main*
glavnik *comb*
glavobol *headache*
gladališče *theatre*
gledati *watch* (vb.)

globok, –a, –o *deep*
gluh, –a, –o *deaf*
goba *mushroom; sponge for cleaning*
golf *golf*
gora *mountain*
gospa *Mrs*
gospod *Mr; sir; gentleman*
gospodar *boss*
gospodična *Miss*
gost *guest*
gotovina *ready cash*
govedina *beef*
govoriti *speak; talk* (vb.)
gozd *forest; woods*
grad *castle*
graditi *build* (vb.)
grah *peas*
gram *gram*
grelec *heater*
gripa *flu*
grlo *throat*
grmeti *thunder*
grozdje *grapes*
gumb *button*

hči *daughter*
hiša *house*
hiter, –tra, –o *fast; quick*
hitro *quickly*
hitrost *speed*
hlače *trousers*
hladen, –dna, –o *cool*
hladilnik *fridge*
hleb *loaf*
hoditi *walk* (vb.); *attend*
hoja *walk* (n.)
hotel *hotel*
hoteti *want*
hrana *food*
hraniti *feed*
hrbet *back*
hrib *hill*
hrupen, –pna, –o *noisy*
hruška *pear*
hvala *thank you*

igra *game*
igrati *play* (vb.)

ime *first name*
imeti *have*
in *and*
injekcija *injection*
informacije *information office; enquiries*
invalid *disabled person*
invalidski voziček *wheelchair*
inženir *engineer*
Irec, Irka (f.) *Irishman, –woman*
Irska *Ireland*
iskati *look for*
Italija *Italy*
Italijan –ka *Italian*
iti *go* (vb.)
iz *from, of*
izbira *choice*
izčrpan, –a, –o *exhausted; run down*
izgubiti *lose* (vb.)
izgubljen, –a, –o *lost*
izhod *exit* (n.)
izklopiti *switch off; turn off*
izlet *trip*
izložba *shop window*
izpit *examination*
izplačati *pay (out)*
izplačati se *to be worthwhile*
izposoditi si *borrow*
izseljenci *emigrants*
izstopiti *get off*

ja *yes*
jabolko *apple*
jagnje *lamb*
jagoda *strawberry*
jahati *ride* (vb.)
jahta *yacht*
jajce *egg*
jasen, –sna, –o *clear* (adj.)
javen, –vna, –o *public*
jaz *I*
je *is* (he, she, it *is*)
jed *meal; dish*
jedilnilist *menu*
jedilni pribor *cutlery*
jedilnica *dining-room*
jesen *autumn*

jesti *eat*
jetra *liver*
jezen, –zna, –o *angry*
jezero *lake*
jezik *tongue; language*
jogurt *yogurt*
jokati *cry* (vb.)
jug *south*
juha *soup*
jutri *tomorrow*
jutro *morning*

kaditi *smoke* (vb.)
kaj *any; what?*
kako *how*
kakorkoli *anyhow; anyway*
kamion *lorry*
kamp *camp*
kamping *campsite*
Kanada *Canada*
karkoli *anything*
kaseta *cassette; tape*
kasetofon *tape-recorder*
kašljati *cough* (vb.)
kasneje *later*
kateri, –a, –o *which (one)*
kava *coffee*
kavarna *café*
kazen *fine* (n.)
kdaj? *when?*
kdo? *who?*
kino *cinema*
kis *vinegar*
kje? *where?*
klicati *call* (vb.)
ključ *key*
klobasa *sausage*
klobuk *hat*
kmalu *soon*
kmetija *farm*
knjiga *book* (n.)
knjigarna *bookshop*
knijigovodja *bookkeeper*
knjižnica *library*
koledar *calendar*
koleno *knee*
kolesariti *cycle* (vb.)
koliko? *how many? how much?*

kolo *bicycle; wheel*
končati *finish* (vb.)
koncert *concert*
konec *end* (n.)
konj *horse*
konzerva *tin*
konzulat *consulate*
kopališče *swimming-pool*
kopalke *swimming-trunks*
kopalnica *bathroom*
korenje *carrots*
koristen, –tna, –o *useful*
kos *piece; slice*
koš *wastebin*
košara *basket*
košarka *basketball*
kosilo *lunch*
kost *bone*
kostanj *chestnut*
kovček *case; suitcase*
koža *skin*
kozarec *drinking-glass*
kralj *king*
kraljica *queen*
kratek, –tka, –o *short*
krava *cow*
kravata *tie* (n.)
kreditna kartica *credit card*
kri *blood*
krilo *skirt*
križanka *crossword puzzle*
križišče *junction* (on a road)
krompir *potato*
krožnik *plate*
kruh *bread*
kuhar *cook* (n.)
kuhinja *kitchen*
kumara *cucumber*
kupiti *buy*

lačen, –čna, –o *hungry*
ladja *ship* (n.)
lahek, –hka, –o *easy*
lahko *be able to; can*
lahko noč *good night*
lasje *hair*
lastnik *owner*
led *ice*
leden, –a, –o *iced*

ledvice *kidneys*
lekarna *chemist's*
len, –a, –o *lazy*
lep, –a, –o *beautiful*
les *wood*
letališče *airport*
letalo *plane*
leteti *fly*
leto *year*
letos *this year*
likalnik *iron*
likati *iron* (vb.)
limona *lemon*
ljubezen *love* (n.)
ljubiti *love* (vb.)
ljudje *people*
losos *salmon*
lubenica *watermelon*
luna *moon*

maček *cat*
majhen, –hna, –o *small*
majica *T-shirt; vest*
malina *raspberry*
malinovec *raspberry juice*
malo *little; a bit*
mama *mother*
marelica *apricot*
margarina *margarine*
marmelada *jam*
maslo *butter*
masten, –tna, –o *greasy*
med *honey*
med *during; between*
med tem ko *while*
medicinska sestra *nurse*
mednarodni, –a, –o
  international
megla *fog*
meglen, –a, –o *foggy; misty*
melancana *aubergine*
melona *melon*
menjalni tečaj *exchange rate*
menjalnica *bureau de change*
mesec *month*
mesnica *butcher's*
meso *meat*
mesto *city; town*
mineralna voda *mineral water*

misliti *think*
miza *table*
mlad, –a, –o *young*
mleko *milk* (n.)
mleto meso *mince* (meat)
močan, –čna, –o *strong*
moda *fashion*
modern, –a, –o *modern*
moder, –dra, –o *blue*
mogoče *maybe; perhaps; possible*
morati *must* (vb.)
morda *maybe; perhaps*
morje *sea*
MOŠKI *men's toilet*
most *bridge*
mož *husband*
mrzel, –zla, –o *cold* (adj.)
mudi se *hurry, to be in a hurry*
muzej *museum*

na *onto; on; to*
nadstropje *floor*
naglas *accent*
nahrbtnik *rucksack*
najemnina *rental*
najeti *hire*
najti *find* (vb.)
nalezljiv, –a, –o *infectious*
namesto *instead*
napačen, –čna, –o *wrong* (adj.)
napaka *flaw; error; mistake*
napitnina *tip*
napoved *forecast*
naravnost *straight on*
narečje *dialect*
narediti *do* (vb.); *make* (vb.)
naslov *address; title*
nasproti *opposite*
na svidenje *goodbye*
natakar *waiter*
natakarica *waitress*
navada *habit, custom*
navadno *usually*
navajen, –a, –o *to be used to, accustomed*
ne *no; not*
nebo *sky*
nečak *nephew*

nečakinja *niece*
nekadilci *non-smokers*
nekaj *few; a few; a bit*
nekdo *someone*
neki, –a, –o *some*
Nemčija *Germany*
Nemec, Nemka (f.) *German*
nenadoma *suddenly*
neposreden, –dna, –o *direct*
nepotrpežljiv, –a, –o *impatient*
nesporazum *misunderstanding*
nesreča *accident*
nesrečen, –čna, –o *unlucky*
nesti; nositi *carry*
neumen, –mna, –o *stupid*
nevaren, –rna, –o *dangerous*
nevihta *storm*
nezaposlen, –a, –o *unemployed*
nezavesten, –tna, –o *unconscious*
nič *zero, nothing*
nihče *nobody*
nikoli *never*
nizek, –zka, –o *low*
noč *night*
noga *leg; foot*
nogomet *football*
nos *nose*
nov, –a, –o *new*
novice *news*
novinar *journalist*
nož *knife*
nujno *urgently*

o *about*
ob *by; at; near*
oba *both*
obala *seaside*
običajno *usually*
obisk *visit*
oblačen, –čna, –o *cloudy*
oblačila *clothes*
obleči (se) *dress (oneself)*
obleka *man's suit; woman's dress*
obraz *face* (n.)
obvestilo *notification; information*
očala *glasses*

oče *father*
ocvrt, –a, –o *fried*
od *from; of*
odbojka *volleyball*
oddelek *department*
odličen, –čna, –o *perfect; excellent*
odpadki *rubbish*
odpovedati *cancel*
odpreti *open* (vb.)
odprt, –a, –o *open* (adj.)
odvetnik *lawyer; solicitor*
ogenj *fire* (n.)
ogledalo *mirror* (n.)
okno *window*
oko *eye*
okoli *about; around*
okus *taste* (n.)
omaka *sauce*
omara *wardrobe*
omleta *omelette*
on *he*
ona *she*
onadva *they two*
oni *they*
opazovati *observe* (vb.)
opoldan *midday*
oprostite! *excuse me; I'm sorry*
oprostiti *forgive*
oranžen, –žna, –o *orange* (adj.)
oseba *person*
ostati *remain; stay*
otok *island*
otroci *children*
otrok *child*
ozek, –zka, –o *narrow*

palačinka *pancake*
papir *paper*
papirnica *stationer's*
par *pair; couple*
paradižnik *tomato*
park *park* (n.)
pas *belt; waist*
pašteta *paté*
pasti *fall* (vb.)
pečen, –a, –o *fried; baked*
pečenka *roast* (n.)
pečica *oven*

pecivo *pastry*
pekarna *bakery*
peljati *drive, lead, take*
pepelnik *ashtray*
peron *platform*
pes *dog*
pesa *beetroot*
pešec *pedestrian*
pesem *song*
peteršilj *parsley*
peti *sing* (vb.)
pijača *drink* (n.)
pikanten, –tna, –o *spicy*
piknik *picnic*
pisarna *office*
pisati *write*
piščanec *chicken*
pismo *letter*
piti *drink* (vb.)
plača *wage, salary*
plačati *pay* (vb.)
plačilo *payment*
plašč *coat*
plavati *swim* (vb.)
plaža *beach*
pločnik *pavement*
po *after; on; by*
počasen, –sna, –o *slow*
počasi *slowly*
poceni *cheap*
počitnice *holiday*
počivati *rest* (vb.)
pod *under*
podjetje *company*
podoben, –bna, –o *similar*
podpis *signature*
pogledati *take a look*
pogoj *condition*
pogost, –a, –o *frequent*
pogosto *often*
pogovor *conversation; talk* (n.)
pohištvo *furniture*
pokazati *show* (vb.)
poklicati *call* (vb.)
pol *half*
policija *police*
poljub *kiss* (n.)
poljubiti *kiss* (vb.)
polovica *half*

pomagati *help* (vb.)
pomemben, –bna, –o *important*
pomivalni stroj *dishwasher*
pomlad *spring* (n. -season)
pomoč *help; aid; assistance*
ponoviti *repeat* (vb.)
ponudba *offer* (n.)
poper *pepper*
popoldan *afternoon*
popust *discount*
poslati *post* (vb.); *send* (vb.)
poslušati *listen* (to)
posoditi *lend*
pošta *post-office*
postaja *station*
postajališče taksijev *taxi rank*
postati *become*
postaviti *put; place* (vb.)
postelja *bed*
poštna številka *postcode*
poštni nabiralnik *post box;*
  letterbox
postrežba *service*
postrežba v sobo *room service*
postrežček *porter*
postrv *trout*
posušiti *dry* (vb.)
pot *way; path*
potni list *passport*
potnik, potnica (f.) *passenger*
potovalni čeki *traveller's*
  cheques
potovanje *journey*
potovati *travel* (vb.)
povabilo *invitation*
povabiti *invite*
povedati *tell; let know*
povratna vozovnica *return*
  ticket
pozabiti *forget*
pozdravljeni! *hello!*
pozen, –zna, –o *late*
pralni stroj *washing machine*
prav *OK*
praznik *public holiday*
preden *before*
predjed *starter* (at a meal)
predstava *performance; show*
  (n.)

prehod za pešce *pedestrian*
  crossing
prej *before; previously*
prejšnji, –a, –e *former*
premisliti *think over*
prenočišče *accommodation*
prepovedan, –a, –o *prohibited*
prepričan, –a, –o *certain; sure*
prevesti *translate*
prevod *translation*
prha *shower* (n.)
pri *by; at*
prihod *arrival*
priimek *surname*
prijatelj-ica (f.) *friend*
prijaviti *declare*
prijeten, –tna, –o *pleasant; nice*
priložnost *opportunity; chance*
primer *example*
prinesti *bring*
pripraviti *prepare*
prispeti *arrive*
priti *come*
pritličje *ground floor*
prižgati *switch on; turn on*
priznati *admit; acknowledge*
prodajalec –lka (f.) *shop*
  assistant
prodati; prodajati *sell* (vb.)
program *programme*
promet *traffic*
prosim *please*
prosto *vacant*
proti *against* (prep.)
prst *finger*
prtljaga *luggage*
prvi, –a, –o *first*
prva pomoč *first aid*
pulover *pullover*

račun *bill; receipt; invoice*
računovodja *accountant*
rad, –a *like* (vb.)
radio *radio*
razdalja *distance*
razen *except*
razgled *view* (n.)
razglednica *postcard*
razočaran, –a, –o *disappointed*

razprodaja *sales*
razstava *exhibition; display* (n.)
razumeti *understand*
rdeč, –a, –e *red*
recepcija *reception*
recept *doctor's prescription;
cooking recipe*
receptor, –ka *receptionist*
reči *say* (vb.)
reka *river*
reklama *advertisement*
restavracija *restaurant*
rezati *cut* (vb.)
rezervacija *booking; reservation*
rezervirano *reserved*
rezervirati *reserve; book* (vb.)
riba *fish* (n.)
rjav, –a, –o *brown*
rojstni dan *birthday*
roka *hand; arm*
rokavice *gloves*
roza *pink*
rumen, –a, –o *yellow*

s *with*
sadje *fruit*
sadni sok *fruit juice*
samo *only*
samopostrežna *self-service
(shop)*
sandali *sandals*
sardina *sardine*
sedaj *now*
sedeti *sit*
semafor *traffic lights*
sendvič *sandwich*
servieta *napkin; serviette*
sesalec *vacuum-cleaner*
sestra *sister*
sever *north*
Severna Irska *Northern Ireland*
sin *son*
sir *cheese*
siv, –a, –o *grey*
skakati *jump* (vb.)
skodelica *cup*
skoraj *almost*
skozi *through*
skrbeti *worry* (vb.)

skupaj *together*
skupina *group*
slab, –a, –o *bad*
sladek, –dka, –o *sweet* (adj.)
sladica *pudding; sweet*
sladkor *sugar*
sladoled *ice cream*
slanina *bacon*
slaven, –vna, –o *famous*
slediti *follow*
slika *picture, painting*
slišati *hear*
sliva *plum*
slovar *dictionary*
služba *job*
smer *direction; route*
smešen, –šna, –o *funny*
smeti *rubbish*
smetnjak *dustbin*
sneg *snow*
snežiti *snow* (vb.)
soba *room*
sok *fruit juice; squash*
sol *salt*
solata *salad*
sonce *sun*
sončen, –čna, –o *sunny*
sončna očala *sunglasses*
sosed, –a *neighbour*
spalna vreča *sleeping bag*
spalnica *bedroom*
spati *sleep* (vb.)
spodaj *down; downstairs;
below*
spominki *gift-shop*
spomniti se *remember*
sporočilo *message; information*
spoznati *meet*
srajca *shirt*
srce *heart*
sreča *luck*
središče *centre*
stanovanje *flat; apartment*
stanovati *live* (vb.)
star, –a, –o *old*
starši *parents*
steklenica *bottle*
stol *chair*
stopnice *stairs*

storiti *do; make* (vb.)
stranišče *toilet*
stric *uncle*
strinjati se *agree*
svet *world*
svetovati *recommend*
svež, –a, –e *fresh*
svinčnik *pencil*
svinjina *pork*

šal *shawl, scarf*
še *more; yet*
šef *boss*
šibek, –bka, –o *weak*
širok, –a, –o *wide*
škatla *box*
školjke *shellfish*
škornji *boots*
Škot *Scotsman*
Škotinja *Scotswoman*
Škotska *Scotland*
šola *school*
šotor *tent*
Španija *Spain*
špinača *spinach*
štedilnik *cooker*
številka *number, size for clothes*
študent *student*
šunka *ham*
Švica *Switzerland*

ta *this*
tableta *tablet*
tako *so*
takoj *immediately*
taksi *taxi; cab*
tašča *mother-in-law*
tast *father-in-law*
teden *week*
telefon *telephone*
telefonirati *telephone* (vb.)
teletina *veal*
televizija *television*
telo *body*
temen, –mna, –o *dark*
temperatura *temperature*
tenis *tennis*
terasa *terrace*

testenine *pasta*
teta *aunt*
težek, –žka, –o *hard; heavy; difficult*
ti *you* (sg.)
tih, –a, –o *quiet*
tla *floor*
topel, –pla, –o *warm*
torba *bag*
torta *cake*
tovarna *factory*
trafika *tobacconist's*
trebuh *stomach*
trg *square*
trgovec, –vka (f.) *shop assistant*
trgovina *shop*
tržnica *market*
tudi *also*
tukaj *here*
turist *tourist*
tuš *shower* (n.)

učitelj, –ica (f.) *teacher*
učiti *teach*
učiti se *learn*
udoben, –bna, –o *comfortable*
ugasniti *switch off; turn off*
ulica *street*
umazan, –a, –o *dirty*
umiti *wash* (vb.)
umiti se *wash oneself*
umivalnik *washbasin*
upati *hope* (vb.)
ura *watch; hour; clock*
usta *mouth*
ustaviti *stop* (vb.)
utrujen, –a, –o *tired*

v *in; into*
vagon *carriage (train)*
vas *village*
včasih *sometimes*
včeraj *yesterday*
več *more*
večer *evening*
večerja *supper; evening meal*
vedeti *know*
vedno *always*
veleblagovnica *department store*

veleposlaništvo *embassy*
velik, –a, –o *large; big*
velika noč *Easter*
veliko *several; many; a lot; much*
verjeti *believe*
verjetno *probably*
ves, vsa, vso *whole; all; total*
vesel, –a, –o *happy*
veter *wind* (n.)
vi *you* (pl.)
videti *see* (vb.)
vidva *you two*
vilica *fork* (for eating)
vino *wine* (n.)
visok, –a, –o *tall*
vklopiti *turn on; switch on*
vlak *train*
vključen, –čna, –o *included*
voda *water*
visok, –a, –o *high*
voziti *drive* (vb.)
vozniško dovoljenje *driving licence*
vprašanje *question* (n.)
vprašati *ask* (vb.)
vrat *neck*
vrata *door, gate*
vreme *weather*
vremenska napoved *weather forecast*
vroč, –a, –e *hot*
vrsta *queue* (n.)
vrt *garden*
vsak *every*
vsakdo *everyone*
vse *everything*
vsota *amount*
vzhod *east*
vzrok *reason* (n.)
vstop *entrance*
vstopiti *enter, get in*
vstopnica *entrance ticket*

WC *lavatory*

z *with*
za *for*
zabava *party*

začasno *temporary*
začeti *begin*
zadnji, –a, –e *last* (adj.)
zahod *west*
zajtrk *breakfast*
zakaj *why*
zamenjati *exchange; change* (vb.)
zamuda *delay* (n.)
zamuditi *miss* (vb.)
zanesljiv, –a, –o *reliable*
zanimiv, –a, –o *interesting*
zaprt, –a, –o *closed; shut* (adj.)
zaseden, –a, –o *busy; engaged*
zaskrbljen, –a, –o *worried*
zaspan, –a, –o *sleepy*
zato *because*
zato ker *because*
zdravnik *doctor*
Združene države Amerika *United States of America*
zebe me *I'm cold*
zelen, –a, –o *green*
zelenjava *vegetables*
zelje *cabbage*
zelo *very*
zemljevid *map*
zgodaj *early*
zgoditi se *happen*
zgoraj *upstairs*
zgradba *building*
zima *winter*
zlato *gold*
zmeraj *always*
zmrzovalnik *freezer*
znati *can* (vb.)
zob *tooth*
zobje *teeth*
zobozdravnik, –nica (f.) *dentist*
zrezek *steak, chop*
zvečer *in the evening*

žalosten, –tna, –o *sad*
že *already*
žejen, –jna, –o sem *I'm thirsty*
železniška postaja *railway station*
želodec *stomach*
žemlja *bread roll*

žena *wife*
ŽENSKE *women's toilet*
živalski vrt *zoo*
živeti *live* (vb.)
življenje *life*
žlica *spoon*
žlička *teaspoon*
žoga *ball*

English–Slovene glossary

a bit malo
about o
accent naglas (m.)
accident nesreča (f.)
accommodation prenočišče (n.)
accountant računovodja (m.)
accustomed navajen, -a, -o
ache (vb.) boleti
acknowledge priznati
across čez
add (vb.) dodati
address naslov (m.)
admit priznati
advertisement reklama (f.)
after po
after (time) čez
afternoon popoldan (m.)
against proti
agree strinjati se
agreement dogovor (m.)
aid pomoč (f.)
airport letališče (n.)
alarm clock budilka (f.)
all ves, vsa, vso
allow dovoliti
almost skoraj
already že
also tudi
always vedno; zmeraj
America Amerika (f.)
American Američan (m.), -ka (f.)
amount vsota (f.)
and in

angry jezen, -zna, -o
anyhow kakorkoli
anything karkoli
anyway kakorkoli
apartment apartma (m.); stanovanje (n.)
aperitif aperitiv (m.)
apple jabolko (n.)
apricot marelica (f.)
arm roka (f.)
arrival prihod (m.)
arrive prispeti
artichoke artičoka (f.)
article članek (m.)
ashtray pepelnik (m.)
ask vprašati
asparagus beluš (m.)
aspirin aspirin (m.)
assistance pomoč (f.)
at ob; pri
at home doma
attend (vb.) hoditi
aubergine melancana (f.)
aunt teta (f.)
Australia Avstralija (f.)
author avtor (m.), -ica (f.)
automatic avtomatičen, -čna, -o
autumn jesen (f.)

back hrbet (m.)
bacon slanina (f.)
bad slab, -a, -o
bag torba (f.)
baked pečen, -a, -o

bakery pekarna (f.)	*bookkeeper* knjigovodja (m.)
balcony balkon (m.)	*bookshop* knjigarna (f.)
ball žoga (f.)	*boots* škornji (m.)
banana banana (f.)	*boring* dolgočasen, -sna, -o
bank banka (f.)	*borrow* izposoditi si
bank account bančni račun (m.)	*boss* gospodar (m.); šef (m.)
bar bar (m.)	*bottle* steklenica (f.)
barber brivec (m.)	*box* škatla (f.)
basket košara (f.)	*boy* fant (m.)
basketball košarka (f.)	*boyfriend* fant (m.)
bathroom kopalnica (f.)	*bread* kruh (m.)
battery baterija (f.)	*breakfast* zajtrk (m.)
be able to lahko	*bridge* most (m.)
beach plaža (f.)	*briefcase* aktovka (f.)
beans fižol (m.)	*bring* prinesti
beautiful lep, -a, -o	*Britain* Britanija (f.)
because zato (ker)	*brochure* brošura (f.)
become postati	*brother* brat (m.)
bed postelja (f.)	*brown* rjav, -a, -o
bedroom spalnica (f.)	*buffet* bife (m.)
to be in a hurry mudi se	*build* graditi
to be used to navajen, -a, -o	*building* zgradba (f.)
to be worthwhile izplačati se	*bureau de change* menjalnica (f.)
bee čebela (f.)	*bus* avtobus (m.)
beef govedina (f.)	*bus-station, bus-stop* avtobusna
beetroot pesa (f.)	postaja (f.)
before preden; prej	*busy* zaseden, -a, -o
begin začeti	*but* ampak
believe verjeti	*butcher's* mesnica (f.)
below spodaj	*butter* maslo (n.)
better (than) bolje (kot)	*button* gumb (m.)
between med	*buy* kupiti
bicycle kolo (n.)	*by* ob; pri
big velik, -a, -o	
bill račun (m.)	*cab* taksi (m.)
bin koš (m.)	*cabbage* zelje (n.)
binoculars daljnogled (m.)	*café* kavarna (f.)
birthday rojstni dan (m.)	*cake* torta (f.)
black črn, -a, -o	*calendar* koledar (m.)
blood kri (f.)	*call (vb.)* klicati; poklicati
blouse bluza (f.)	*camera* fotoaparat (m.)
blue moder, -dra, -o	*camp* kamp (m.)
boat čoln (m.)	*campsite* kamping (m.)
boat-house čolnarna (f.)	*can (vb.)* lahko; znati
body telo (n.)	*Canada* Kanada (f.)
bone kost (f.)	*car* avto (m.)
book knjiga (f.)	*carrots* korenje (n.)
book (vb.) rezervirati	*carry* nesti; nositi
booking rezervacija (f.)	*cash desk* blagajna (f.)

cassette kaseta (f.)
castle grad (m.)
cat maček (m.)
cauliflower cvetača (f.)
centre središče (n.)
certain prepričan, -a, -o
chair stol (m.)
chance priložnost (f.)
change (vb.) zamenjati
charge cena (f.)
cheap poceni
cheaper ceneje
cheese sir (m.)
cheque ček (m.)
cheque book čekovna knjižica (f.)
cherry češnja (f.)
chestnut kostanj (m.)
chicken piščanec (m.)
chocolate čokolada (f.)
choice izbira (f.)
Christmas božič (m.)
church cerkev (f.)
cigar cigara (f.)
cigarette cigareta (f.)
cinema kino (m.)
city mesto (n.)
clean (adj.) čist, -a, -o
clean (vb.) čistiti
clear jasen, -sna, -o
cloakroom garderoba (f.)
clock ura (f.)
closed zaprt, -a, -o
clothes oblačila (n. pl.)
cloudy oblačen, -čna, -o
coach avtobus (m.)
coat plašč (m.)
coffee kava (f.)
cold (adj.) mrzel, -zla, -o
colour barva (f.)
comb glavnik (m.)
come priti
comfortable udoben, -bna, -o
company firma (f.); podjetje (n.)
concert koncert (m.)
condition pogoj (m.)
congratulations čestitke (f. pl.)
consulate konzulat (m.)
conversation pogovor (m.)

cook kuhar (m.)
cooker štedilnik (m.)
cool hladen, -dna, -o
cost cena (f.)
cotton bombaž (m.)
cough (vb.) kašljati
country dežela (f.); država (f.)
cow krava (f.)
credit card kreditna kartica (f.)
crossword puzzle križanka (f.)
cry (vb.) jokati
cucumber kumara (f.)
cup skodelica (f.)
custom navada (f.)
customs carina (f.)
cut (vb.) rezati
cutlery jedilni pribor (m.)
cycle (vb.) kolesariti

daily dneven, -vna, -o
dangerous nevaren, -rna, -o
dark temen, -mna, -o
date datum (m.)
daughter hči (f.)
day dan (m.)
deaf gluh, -a, -o
dear drag, -a, -o
debt dolg (m.)
declare prijaviti
deep globok, -a, -o
delay zamuda (f.)
delicatessen delikatese (f. pl.)
dentist zobozdravnik (m.),
    zobozdravnica (f.)
department store veleblagovnica
    (f.)
dialect narečje (n.)
diarrhoea driska (f.)
dictionary slovar (m.)
diet dijeta (f.)
different drugačen, -čna, -o
difficult težak, -žka, -o
dining-room jedilnica (f.)
direct neposreden, -dna, -o
direction smer (f.)
dirty umazan, -a, -o
disabled person invalid (m.)
disappointed razočaran, -a, -o
discount popust (m.)

dish jed (f.)
dishwasher pomivalni stroj (m.)
display razstava (f.)
distance razdalja (f.)
do (vb.) storiti; delati; narediti
doctor zdravnik (m.)
documents dokumenti (m.)
dog pes (m.)
dollar dolar (m.)
door vrata (n. pl.)
doubt dvom (m.); (vb.) dvomiti
down dol; spodaj
downstairs spodaj
dress (oneself) obleči se
drink pijača (f.); (vb.) piti
drinking-glass kozarec (m.)
drive (vb.) peljati; voziti
driving licence vozniško
dovoljenje
dry (vb.) posušiti
dry cleaner's čistilnica (f.)
during med
dustbin smetnjak (m.)

early zgodaj
east vzhod (m.)
Easter velika noč
easy lahek, -hka, -o
eat jesti
egg jajce (n.)
egg-white beljak (m.)
electric električen, -čna, -o
electrician električar (m.)
electricity elektrika (f.)
embassy veleposlaništvo (n.)
emigrants izseljenci (m.)
end konec (m.)
engaged zaseden, -a, -o
engineer inženir (m.)
England Anglija (f.)
English pound funt (m.)
Englishman, -woman Anglež
(m.), -inja (f.)
enough dovolj
enquiries informacije (f.)
enter vstopiti
entrance vstop (m.)
error napaka (f.)
evening večer (m.)

every vsak
everyone vsakdo
everything vse
examination izpit (m.)
example primer (m.)
except razen
exchange (vb.) zamenjati
exchange rate menjalni tečaj
(m.)
exhausted izčrpan, -a, -o
exhibition razstava (f.)
exit izhod (m.)
expensive drag, -a, -o

face obraz (m.)
factory tovarna (f.)
family družina (f.)
famous slaven, -vna, -o
far daleč
farm kmetija (f.)
fashion moda (f.)
fast hiter, -tra, -o
fat (person) debel, -a, -o
father ata (m.)
father-in-law tast (m.)
feed (vb.) hraniti
festival festival (m.)
few; a few nekaj
film (also roll for camera) film
(m.)
find (vb.) najti
fine kazen (f.)
finger prst (m.)
finish (vb.) končati
fire brigade gasilci (m. pl.)
firm firma (f.)
first prvi, -a, -o
first aid prva pomoč (f.)
first name ime (n.)
fish riba (f.)
flat stanovanje (n.)
flaw napaka (f.)
floor nadstropje (n.); tla (n. pl.)
flu gripa (f.)
fly (vb.) leteti
fog megla (f.)
foggy meglen, -a,-o
follow slediti
food hrana (f.)

foot noga (f.)
football nogomet
for za
forecast napoved (f.)
forest gozd (m.)
forget pozabiti
fork vilica (f.)
former prejšnji, -a, -o
France Francija (f.)
free of charge brezplačen, -čna,-o
freezer zmrzovalnik (m.)
Frenchman, -woman Francoz, (m.) -inja (f.)
frequent pogost, -a, -o
fresh svež, -a, -e
fridge hladilnik (m.)
fried pečen, -a, -o
friend prijatelj (m.), prijateljica (f.)
from iz
fruit sadje (n.)
fruit juice sadni sok (m.); sok (m.)
funny smešen, -šna, -o
furniture pohištvo (n.)

gallery galerija (f.)
game igra (f.)
garage garaža (f.)
garden vrt (m.)
garlic česen (m.)
gate vrata (n. pl.)
gentleman gospod (m.)
German Nemec (m.), Nemka (f.)
Germany Nemčija (f.)
get (obtain) dobiti
get in vstopiti
get off izstopiti
gift darilo (n.)
gift-shop spominki (m. pl.)
girl dekle (n.)
give dati
glasses očala (n.)
gloves rokavice (f.)
go (vb.) iti
God Bog (m.)
gold zlato (n.)

golf golf (m.)
good dober, -bra, -o
good night lahko noč
goodbye na svidenje
gram gram (m.)
grapes grozdje (n.)
greasy masten, -tna, -o
green zelen, -a, -o
grey siv, -a, -o
ground floor pritličje (n.)
group skupina (f.)
guest gost (m.)

habit navada (f.)
hair lasje (m. pl.)
hairdresser frizer (m.)
hairdryer fen (m.)
half pol; polovica (f.)
ham šunka (f.)
hand roka (f.)
happen zgoditi se
happy vesel, -a, -o
hard težak, -žka, -o
hat klobuk (m.)
have imeti
head glava (f.)
headache glavobol (m.)
hear slišati
heart srce (n.)
heater grelec (m.)
heavy težak, -žka, -o
hello! pozdravljeni!
help pomoč (f.)
help (vb.) pomagati
here tukaj
high visok, -a, -o
hill hrib (m.)
hire (vb.) najeti
holiday dopust (m.); počitnice (f. pl.)
home dom (m.)
homesick domotožje (n.)
honey med (m.)
hope (vb.) upati
horse konj (m.)
hospital bolnišnica (f.)
hot vroč, -a, -e
hotel hotel (m.)
hour ura (f.)

house hiša (f.)
how kako
how many? koliko?
how much? koliko?
hungry lačen, -čna, -o
hurt boleti
husband mož (m.)

I jaz
I am cold zebe me
ice led (m.)
ice cream sladoled (m.)
icy leden, -a, -o
if če
ill bolan, -a, -o
immediately takoj
impatient nepotrpežljiv, -a, -o
important pomemben, -bna, -o
in the evening zvečer
in(to) v
included vključen, -a, -o
infectious nalezljiv, -a, -o
information obvestilo (n.);
   sporočilo (n.)
information office informacije
   (f. pl.)
injection injekcija (f.)
instead namesto
interesting zanimiv, -a, -o
international mednarodni, -a, -o
invitation povabilo (n.)
invite povabiti
invoice račun (m.)
Ireland Irska (f.)
Irishman, -woman Irec, Irka
iron likalnik (m.)
iron (vb.) likati
is (he, she, it) je
Italian Italijan (m.), Italijanka (f.)
Italy Italija (f.)

jam marmelada (f.)
job služba (f.)
journalist novinar (m.)
journey potovanje (n.)
jump (vb.) skakati
junction (on the road) križišče
   (n.)

key ključ (m.)
kidneys ledvice (f.)
king kralj (m.)
kiss (n.) poljub (m.)
kiss (vb.) poljubiti
kitchen kuhinja (f.)
knee koleno (n.)
knife nož (m.)
know vedeti

lace čipka (f.)
lake jezero
lamb jagnje (n.)
language jezik (m.)
large velik, -a, -o
last zadnji, -a, -e
late pozen, -zna, -o
later kasneje
lawyer advokat (m.)
lazy len, -a, -o
lead (vb.) peljati
learn učiti se
left-luggage office garderoba (f.)
leg noga (f.)
lemon limona (f.)
lemon tea čaj (m.) z limono
lend posoditi
length dolžina (f.)
let dovoliti
let know povedati
letter pismo (n.)
letterbox poštni nabiralnik (m.)
letter of alphabet črka (f.)
library knjižnica (f.)
life življenje (n.)
lift dvigalo (n.)
lightning bliskanje (n.)
like (vb.) rad, -a, -o; imeti
listen (to) poslušati
little malo
live (vb.) stanovati; živeti
liver jetra (n. pl.)
living-room dnevna soba (f.)
loaf hleb (m.)
long dolg, -a, -o
look at pogledati
look for iskati
lorry kamion (m.)

lose izgubiti
lost izgubljen, -a, -o
loud glasen, -sna, -o
lounge dnevna soba (f.)
love ljubezen (f.)
love (vb.) ljubiti
low nizek, -zka, -o
luck sreča (f.)
luggage prtljaga (f.)
lunch kosilo (n.)

main glavni, -vna, -o
make (vb.) narediti; storiti
man's suit obleka (f.)
manager direktor (m.)
many veliko
map zemljevid (m.)
margarine margarina (f.)
market tržnica (f.)
maybe morda, mogoče
meal obed (m.)
meat meso (n.)
meet spoznati
melon melona (f.)
member član (m.)
men's toilet MOŠKI
menu jedilni list (m.)
message sporočilo (n.)
milk mleko (n.)
mince meat mleto meso (n.)
mineral water mineralna voda (f.)
Miss gospodična (f.)
miss (vb.) zamuditi
mistake napaka (f.)
misty meglen, -a, -o
misunderstanding nesporazum (m.)
money denar (m.)
money: change (n.) drobiž (m.)
month mesec (m.)
moon luna (f.)
more še; več
morning jutro (n.)
mother mama (f.)
mother-in-law tašča (f.)
motorway avtocesta (f.)
mountain gora (f.)
mouth usta (n. pl.)

Mr. gospod (m.)
Mrs. gospa (f.)
much veliko
museum muzej (m.)
mushroom goba (f.)
music glasba (f.)
must morati

napkin servieta (f.)
nationality državljanstvo (n.)
near blizu; ob
neck vrat (m.)
neighbour sosed (m.)
nephew nečak (m.)
never nikoli
new nov, -a, -o
news novice (f.)
newspaper časopis (m.)
nice prijeten, -tna, -o
niece nečakinja (f.)
night noč (f.)
no; not ne
nobody nihče
noisy hrupen, -pna, -o
non-smokers nekadilci (m.)
north sever (m.)
Northern Ireland Severna Irska (f.)
nose nos (m.)
note-pad beležka (f.)
nothing nič
notification obvestilo (n.)
now sedaj
number številka (f.)
nurse medicinska sestra (f.)

of iz
offer ponudba (f.)
office pisarna (f.)
often pogosto
OK prav; v redu
old star, -a, -o
once enkrat
one eden; en
onion čebula (f.)
only samo
onto; on; to na
opportunity priložnost (f.)
opposite nasproti

or ali; can also indicate a question
other drugi, -a, -o
oven pečica (f.)
owe dolgovati
owner lastnik (m.)

pain bolečina (f.)
painting slika (f.)
parents starši (m.)
parsley peteršilj (m.)
part del (m.)
party zabava (f.)
passenger potnik (m.), potnica (f.)
passport potni list (m.)
pasta testenine (f. pl.)
pastry pecivo (n.)
path pot (f.)
pavement pločnik (m.)
pay (out) izplačati
pay (vb.) plačati
payment plačilo (n.)
peach breskev (f.)
pear hruška (f.)
peas grah (m.)
pedestrian pešec (m.)
pedestrian crossing prehod za pešce (m.)
pencil svinčnik (m.)
people ljudje (m.)
pepper poper (m.)
performance predstava (f.)
perhaps morda, mogoče
permit (vb.) dovoliti
person človek (m.)
petrol bencin (m.)
pharmacy lekarna (f.)
photocopy (vb.) fotokopirati
photograph fotografija (f.)
picnic piknik (m.)
picture slika (f.)
piece kos (m.)
pineapple ananas (m.)
pink roza
place (vb.) postaviti
plane letalo (n.)
plate krožnik (m.)
platform peron (m.)

play (vb.) igrati
pleasant prijeten, -tna, -o
please prosim
plum sliva (f.)
police policija (f.)
pork svinjina (f.)
porter postrežček (m.)
possible morda, mogoče
post (vb.) poslati
postcard razglednica (f.)
postcode poštna številka (f.)
post-office pošta (f.)
potato krompir (m.)
prepare pripraviti
prescription recept (m.)
present darilo (n.)
previously prej
price cena (f.)
price list cenik (m.)
priest duhovnik (m.)
probably verjetno
programme program (m.)
prohibited prepovedan, -a, -o
pub bar (m.)
public javen, -vna, -o
public holiday državni praznik (m.)
pudding sladica (f.)
pullover pulover (m.)
purse denarnica (f.)
put postaviti

queen kraljica (f.)
question vprašanje (n.)
queue vrsta (f.)
quick hiter, -tra, -o
quickly hitro
quiet tih, -a, -o

radio radio (m.)
railway station železniška postaja (f.)
rain dež (m.)
raincoat dežni plašč (m.)
raining: it's raining dežuje
raspberry malina (f.)
raspberry juice malinovec (m.)
read (vb.) brati
ready cash gotovina (f.)

reason vzrok (m.)
receipt račun (m.)
reception recepcija (f.)
receptionist receptor (m.), -ka (f.)
recipe recept (m.)
recommend svetovati
red rdeč, -a, -o
reliable zanesljiv, -a, -o
remember spomniti se
rental najemnina (f.)
repeat (vb.) ponoviti
reservation rezervacija (f.)
reserve (vb.) rezervirati
reserved rezervirano
rest (vb.) počivati
restaurant restavracija (f.)
return ticket povratna vozovnica (f.)
rich bogat, -a, -o
ride (vb.) jahati
river reka (f.)
road cesta (f.)
roast pečenka (f.)
roll (of bread) žemlja (f.)
room soba (f.)
room service postrežba v sobo (f.)
route smer (f.)
rubbish smeti (f. pl.)
rucksack nahrbtnik (m.)
run down izčrpan, -a, -o

sad žalosten, -tna, -o
salad solata (f.)
salary plača (f.)
sales razprodaja (f.)
salmon losos (m.)
salt sol (f.)
sandals sandali (m.)
sandwich sendvič (m.)
sardine sardina (f.)
sausage klobasa (f.)
say (vb.) reči
scarf šal (m.)
school šola (f.)
Scotland Škotska (f.)
Scotsman Škot (m.)
Scotswoman Škotinja (f.)

sea morje (n.)
seaside obala (f.)
second drugi, -a, -o
see videti
self-service (shop) samopostrežna (f.)
sell prodati; prodajati
send poslati
service postrežba (f.)
serviette servieta (f.)
several veliko
shave (vb.) briti
shawl šal (m.)
shellfish školjke (f. pl.)
ship ladja (f.)
shirt srajca (f.)
shock absorber blažilec (m.)
shoe čevelj (m.)
shop trgovina (f.)
shop assistant trgovec (m.), trgovka (f.); prodajalec (m.), prodajalka (f.)
shop window izložba (f.)
short kratek, -tka, -o
show predstava (f.)
show (vb.) pokazati
shower prha (f.); tuš (m.)
shut zaprt, -a, -o
shut (vb.) zapreti
sick bolan, -lna, -o
signature podpis (m.)
similar podoben, -bna, -o
sing (vb.) peti
sir gospod (m.)
sister sestra (f.)
sit sedeti
size of clothes številka (f.)
skin koža (f.)
skirt krilo (n.)
sky nebo (n.)
sleep (vb.) spati
sleeping bag spalna vreča (f.)
sleepy zaspan, -a, -o
slice kos (m.)
slippers copati (m.)
slow počasen, -sna, -o
slowly počasi
small majhen, -hna, -o
smoke (vb.) kaditi

snack bar bife (m.)
snow sneg (m.)
snow (vb.) snežiti
so tako
solicitor advokat (m.)
some neki, -a, -o
someone nekdo
sometimes včasih
son sin (m.)
song pesem (f.)
soon kmalu
soup juha (f.)
south jug (m.)
Spain Španija (f.)
speak govoriti
speed hitrost (f.)
spicy pikanten, -tna, -o
spinach špinača (f.)
sponge (for cleaning) goba (f.)
spoon žlica (f.)
spring pomlad (f.)
square trg (m.)
squash sok (m.)
stairs stopnice (f.)
starter (at a meal) predjed (f.)
station postaja (f.)
steak zrezek (m.)
stew enolončnica (f.)
stomach trebuh (m.); želodec (m.)
stop (vb.) ustaviti
storm nevihta (f.)
straight on naravnost
strawberry jagoda (f.)
street ulica (f.)
strong močan, -čna, -o
student študent (m.); študentka (f.)
stupid neumen, -mna, -o
suddenly nenadoma
sugar sladkor (m.)
suitcase kovček (m.)
sun sonce (n.)
sunglasses sončna očala (n.)
sunny sončen, -čna, -o
supper večerja (f.)
supplement dodatek (m.)
sure prepričan, -a, -o
surname priimek (m.)
sweet sladek, -dka, -o

swim (vb.) plavati
swimming-pool plavalni bazen (m.)
swimming-trunks kopalke (f.)
switch off izklopiti; ugasniti
switch on prižgati; vklopiti
Switzerland Švica (f.)

table miza (f.)
tablet tableta (f.)
take (vb.) peljati
take photographs fotografirati
talk (vb.) govoriti
tall visok, -a, -o
tape kaseta (f.)
tape-recorder kasetofon (m.)
tax davek (m.)
taxi taksi (m.)
taxi rank postajališče taksijev (n.)
tea čaj (m.)
tea with milk čaj (m.) z mlekom
teach učiti
teacher učitelj, -ica (f.)
teapot čajnik (m.)
teaspoon žlička (f.)
teeth zobje (m.)
telephone telefon (m.)
telephone (vb.) telefonirati
television televizija (f.)
tell povedati
temperature temperatura (f.)
temporary začasno
tennis tenis (m.)
tent šotor (m.)
terrace terasa (f.)
thank you hvala
that (conj.) da
theatre gledališče (n.)
thick (book) debel, -a, -o
think (vb.) misliti
think over premisliti
thirsty žejen, -jna, -o
this ta
this year letos
throat grlo (n.)
through skozi
thunder (vb.) grmeti
ticket vstopnica (f.)
tie kravata (f.)

till (cash desk)   blagajna (f.)
till (conj.)   do
time čas (m.)
tin konzerva (f.)
tip napitnina (f.)
tired utrujen, -a, -o
title naslov (m.)
tobacconist's   trafika (f.)
today danes
together skupaj
toilet stranišče (n.); WC
tomorrow jutri
tongue jezik (m.)
tooth zob (m.)
total cel, -a, -o; ves, vsa, vso
tourist turist (m.)
towel brisača (f.)
town mesto (n.)
traffic promet (m.)
traffic lights semafor (m.)
train vlak (m.)
train carriage vagon (m.)
translate prevesti
translation prevod (m.)
travel (vb.) potovati
traveller's cheques potovalni
   čeki (m.)
tree drevo (n.)
trip izlet (m.)
trousers hlače (f.)
trout postrv (f.)
T-shirt majica (f.)
turn off izklopiti; ugasniti
turn on prižgati; vklopiti
twice dvakrat

umbrella dežnik (m.)
uncle stric (m.)
unconscious nezavesten, -tna, -o
under pod
understand razumeti
unemployed nezaposlen, -a, -o
United States of America
   Združene Države Amerike (f.)
unlucky nesrečen, -čna, -o
upstairs zgoraj
urgently nujno
useful koristen, -tna, -o
usually navadno; običajno

vacant prosto
vacuum cleaner sesalec (m.)
valley dolina (f.)
veal teletina (f.)
vegetables zelenjava (f.)
very zelo
vest majica (f.)
view razgled (m.)
village vas (f.)
vinegar kis (m.)
visit obisk (m.)
voice glas (m.)

wage plača (f.)
wait (for) čakati (na)
waiter natakar (m.)
waiting-room čakalnica (f.)
waitress natakarica (f.)
walk hoja (f.)
walk (vb.) hoditi
wall zid (m.)
wallet denarnica (f.)
want (vb.) hoteti
warm topel, -pla, -o
wash (vb.) umiti
wash oneself umiti se
washbasin umivalnik (m.)
washing machine pralni stroj
   (m.)
watch ura (f.)
watch (vb.) gledati
water voda (f.)
watermelon lubenica (f.)
way pot (f.), cesta (f.)
weak šibek, -bka, -o
weather vreme (n.)
weather forecast vremenska
   napoved (f.)
week teden (m.)
welcome! dobrodošli!
well dobro
west zahod (m.)
what? kaj?
wheel kolo (n.)
wheelchair invalidski voziček
   (m.)
when kadar, ko
when? kdaj?
where? kje?

which (one) kateri, -a, -o
while medtem ko
white bel, -a, -o
who? kdo?
whole cel, -a, -o; ves, vsa, vso
whose čigav, -a, -o
why zakaj
wide širok, - a, -o
wife žena (f.)
wind veter (m.)
wine vino (n.)
winter zima (f.)
with s; z
without brez
woman's dress obleka (f.)
women's toilet ŽENSKE
wood les (m.)
woods gozd (m.)
word beseda (f.)
work delo (n.)
work (vb.) delati
world svet (m.)
worried zaskrbljen, -a, -o
worry (vb.) skrbeti
write pisati
wrong (adj.) napačen, -čna, -o

yacht jahta (f.)
year leto (n.)
yellow rumen, -a, -o
yes da; ja
yesterday včeraj
yet še
yoghurt jogurt (m.)
you (pl.)   vi
you (sg.)   ti
you two vidva
young mlad, -a, -o

zero nič
zoo živalski vrt (m.)

index to grammar notes

taking it further

Visitors to Slovenia

For information regarding visits to Slovenia, holidays and general information contact:
STIC – Slovenian Tourist Information Centre
Tel: +386 (0)1 306 45 75/76
Fax: +386 (0)1 306 45 80
Email: stic@ljubljana-tourism.si

Language

Hermina Jug-Kranjec: *Slovenščina za tujce*, Narodna in univerzitetna knjižnica, Ljubljana, 1999
Andreja Markovič [et al.]: *S slovenščino nimam težav (nadaljevalna stopnja)*, Narodna in univerzitetna knjižnica, Ljubljana, 2003
Slovenian Phrase Book & Dictionary, Berlitz publishing/APA Publications GmbH & Co. Verlag KG, Singapore Branch, Singapore. Založba Tuma d.o.o., Slovenia – 2004.

Background information

General history

Mark Mazower: *The Balkans, A Short History*, Weidenfeld & Nicholson, London, 2002
Laura Silber and Allan Little: *The Death of Yugoslavia*, BBC Penguin, London, 1996

National history

James Gow and Cathie Carmichael: *Slovenia and the Slovenes*, Indiana University Press, 2000

Travel writing
Zoe Bran: *After Yugoslavia*, Lonely Planet, 2001

Guide books
The Lonely Planet: *Slovenia*, Lonely Planet Publications, Melbourne, Oakland, London, Paris – 2001.
David Robertson and Sarah Stewart: *Slovenia Walks, Car Tours, Picnics*, Sunflower Books, London, 2003